PASSCHENDAELE
1917

PASSCHENDAELE
1917

CHRIS McNAB

First published 2014
This edition published 2015

Spellmount, an imprint of
The History Press
The Mill, Brimscombe Port
Stroud, Gloucestershire, GL5 2QG
www.thehistorypress.co.uk

British Library Cataloguing in Publication Data.
A catalogue record for this book is available from the British Library.

ISBN 978 0 7509 6062 5

Typesetting and origination by The History Press
Printed in India

CONTENTS

ACKNOWLEDGEMENTS

The author would like to thanks all those at The History Press involved with the production of this book. Special thanks go to Jo de Vries, Sophie Bradshaw and Declan Flynn.

INTRODUCTION

The word 'Passchendaele' has a special and sombre resonance in British history. Like the Somme, Passchendaele is a kind of shorthand for the epic suffering of the 'Great War', a term that instantly evokes a picture of terrible human cost and gross destruction for little physical gain. Mention Passchendaele, and grainy images stir in the collective memory – a hopeless, tree-stripped landscape; a bottomless mud, sucking men and even horses to their doom; the rattle of the Vickers and the Maxim; the pounding destruction of shellfire; corpses littered like leaves, and soggy graves waiting to receive them.

The emotions are warranted. Passchendaele was indeed a battle of grievous suffering and questionable achievements. Yet we must be precise about what we mean by 'Passchendaele'. It has become a single term for describing what is actually more properly known as the Third Battle of Ypres, fought in West Flanders between July and November 1917.

The village of Passchendaele itself sat on a strategic ridge to the east of Ypres, and in October–November was the focal point of two major battles at the culmination of the Ypres battle. Such was the horror of these engagements, both in terms of the fighting and the physical environment in which the men clashed, that Passchendaele came to represent more than just its individual actions, but embodied the wider struggle around Ypres in 1917.

In this book, we will look in detail at both the Third Battle of Ypres and the actions around Passchendaele, making a distinction between the two. The story, as we shall see, is as fascinating as it is tragic. Yet the scale of the suffering and loss experienced in those Flanders fields in 1917 means it is a story that makes repeated demands for its retelling.

Ypres

During conflict, it is often the special fate of certain locations to be focal points of unusual levels of prolonged destruction. Between 1914 and 1918, there were several such locations on the Western Front, including the Somme and Verdun, and ranked equally alongside them is the Belgian city of Ypres. An almost permanent battleground over four years of war, Ypres descended from a prosperous commercial town to a blackened, gutted ruin. Five major battles were fought around Ypres, and between those violent episodes shelling and raiding actions rumbled on incessantly.

Why this is so might not be immediately apparent. Ypres (now properly 'Ieper', its official Dutch-language name, although during the war it was known by its French title) sits in the north-western corner of Belgium, roughly 50 miles (80km) west of Brussels in the Flemish province of West Flanders. Ypres in its fullest definition is actually a municipality, consisting of the city of Ypres itself plus a host of outlying villages.

A cursory glance at the map reveals little about why Ypres should be of such strategic importance in the First World War. Ypres' origins stretch back to Roman times and beyond, but it was during the Middle Ages that the city rose to influence, as a major centre for the production and trading of textiles. Through Ypres, cloth was distributed widely to foreign lands, either via overland routes across mainland Europe or sent by ship from the nearby ports of Ostend and Antwerp. On the back of this industry, Ypres grew to be a city of significance on the world stage, rivalling nearby Bruges and Ghent.

Ypres' famous Cloth Hall, seen in pristine condition before the war. German shelling between 1914 and 1918 reduced it to an absolute ruin.

A combination of commercial power and a good strategic location near the Channel ports meant that over the centuries, Ypres became all too familiar with the politics and the bloodshed of war, a fact reflected in the city's regular fortification between the fourteenth and the eighteenth centuries.

Flanders was a well-trodden battleground during the medieval period, fated with clashes such as the Battle of the Golden Spurs (1302) and sieges such as that conducted between May and August 1383, part of the Henry le Despenser's 'Norwich Crusade'. The city was also caught up in the dynastic and religious turmoil of the seventeenth and eighteenth centuries. It was conquered by the French in 1678, passed to the Spanish in 1697 and became part of the Austrian Netherlands in 1713. The French Revolutionary Wars broke the grip of the Habsburgs on the Low Countries, and the Belgian Revolution of 1830 put Ypres under the authority of an independent Belgium.

So, by the time the match of war was struck in Europe in 1914, Ypres had seen and survived centuries of upheaval and continental violence. Yet nothing in its long history would contextualise Ypres' experience of the First World War, for it was Ypres' misfortune to come to occupy a vital strategic spot on the trench-locked Western Front.

To begin with, it stood directly in the path of the German advance delineated by the infamous pre-war Schlieffen Plan. This plan, set down by chief of the imperial German general staff, Count Alfred von Schlieffen in 1904/1905, and later modified by his replacement, Helmuth von Moltke, was nothing less than a German blueprint for a military conquest of Europe. The challenge faced by the Germans was how to handle a two-front war, trapped in a vice between France and Britain to the west and Russia to the east. Schlieffen's solution was essentially to use neutral Belgium, Luxembourg and the Netherlands as a through-route for rapid victory in the west. German forces would invade in a vast and powerful sweep from the north, cutting down through the neutral territories and driving south to encircle Paris and crush the British and French armies. Take France within six weeks, the plan theorised, and Russia would not have enough time to mobilise before the German forces could switch their attention to the Eastern Front.

Count Alfred von Schlieffen, the mastermind of Germany's plan to win a two-front war against Western Europe and Russia. The plan failed in practice when executed in 1914.

In 1906, von Moltke modified the plan somewhat. While keeping the strong sweep from the north, he reduced its strength, focusing more troops into reinforcing border positions, especially in Alsace-Lorraine. He would also avoid using the Netherlands as a route of advance – Belgium and Luxembourg would instead bear the brunt of the initial German thrusts. Ypres sat at the outer extremity of the German push, just to the west of the intended invasion route of von Kluck's First Army of 320,000 men.

After a series of runaway political emergencies in Europe, following the assassination of the Austro-Hungarian Archduke Franz Ferdinand in Sarajevo on 28 June 1914, Germany finally had the chance to put the Schlieffen Plan into effect with the opening of hostilities in Western Europe on 2 August. For Ypres, the war at first swept past to the east, the Germans driving south through central Belgium, taking Brussels on 20 August, and pushing on into northern France against the French Fifth Army and the newly deployed British Expeditionary Force (BEF).

General Helmuth von Moltke, who served as the chief of the German general staff between 1906 and 1914, and who took responsibility for strategic adjustments to the Schlieffen Plan.

But the Schlieffen Plan, so carefully modelled in peacetime, unravelled under the realities of conflict. Logistical failures sapped the energy from the German advance, and valuable manpower that could have been devoted to the advance was filtered off for various consolidation or defensive exigencies along the way. As they drove down towards the Marne, the German armies did not have the required strength or tactical position to swing west of Paris, so went south-east instead, attempting to close the gap that had developed between the First and Second Armies. Yet, then came the 'Miracle on the Marne' – an attack by the French Sixth Army from Paris, stabbing into the German right flank. Combined with a subsequent counter-attack by the BEF and the French Fifth Army on 9 September, the result was that the German forces began a general retreat northwards.

From this point the war took a crucial turn, one that would define its character for the next four years. The German forces eventually stopped their retreat around the Aisne, and put down basic trench systems that blocked British attempts to eject the Axis forces. Yet both sides now saw that there was an open flank to the west, and so began the 'Race to the Sea'. Each side scrambled to outflank the other to the west, extending the defended line of entrenchments as they progressed. Neither side managed to outflank the other, and the eventual outcome – realised in the ground by the end of 1914 – was a front line progressively snaking up towards the Belgian coast. What this meant for the citizens of Ypres was that the war was heading their way in earnest.

TIMELINE

1914

1 August	Germany declares war on Russia
2–3 August	Germany enacts the Schlieffen Plan, invading Luxembourg and Belgium and declaring war on France
5–10 September	German invasion of France stopped at the First Battle of the Marne
September–December	German, British and French forces establish trench networks running from the Channel coast down to Switzerland
19 October–22 November	First Battle of Ypres. Germany fails to take Ypres, and the British maintain a prominent salient around the town

1915

10–13 March	Failed British offensive at Neuve Chapelle
22 April–25 May	Second Battle of Ypres. German forces make offensive against Ypres, forcing the reduction of the salient but failing to take it or the city. The battle also saw the extensive use of poison gas by the Germans
25 September–14 October	First Battle of Loos. Major British offensive that includes British use of poison gas and of the 'creeping' artillery barrage. Costs 50,000 British casualties

1916	19 December	Douglas Haig becomes commander-in-chief of the BEF
	21 February–18 December	The Battle of Verdun. This battle of attrition eventually costs the Germans as many casualties as the French, and by December the German forces had lost all their initial gains
	1 July–18 November	The Battle of the Somme, a British offensive launched to relieve pressure on the French at Verdun. For limited gains the British suffer more than 600,000 casualties. Tanks used for first time in combat
1917	February	German forces on the Western Front, weakened by fighting in 1916, are forced to withdraw back to the Hindenburg Line
	6 April	The United States declares war on Germany
	April–May	A British offensive at Arras and French attack at Chemin des Dames bring little change to the front line positions on the Western Front
	31 July–10 November	Third Battle of Ypres. A major British offensive runs aground in appalling weather and in the face of terrible casualties – 250,000 men are killed or wounded. The German Fourth Army suffers similar casualties. The campaign consists of the following major engagements:
	31 July–2 August	The Battle of Pilckem Ridge
	16–18 August	Battle of Langemarck
	20–25 September	Battle of Menin Road Ridge
	26 September–3 October	Battle of Polygon Wood

1917

4 October	Battle of Broodseinde
9 October	Battle of Poelcappelle
12 October	First Passchendaele
26 October– 10 November	Second Passchendaele
20 November	The British Flanders campaign is officially brought to an end

HISTORICAL
BACKGROUND

In 1914, as war crept across the Flanders landscape, few people in Ypres could have conceived that their streets and fields would remain a battlefield for the next four years. The Third Battle of Ypres, as its name implies, was one of just a series of clashes fought for the same locale, events separated by time but not by distance. To comprehend the battle that occurred in 1917, we also need to understand the major battles for Ypres that preceded it.

First Ypres

The First Battle of Ypres (more commonly known by its compressed form, 'First Ypres') was in many ways the culmination of the Race to the Sea (roughly 17 September–19 October 1914). As the scramble unfolded, the area around Ypres was in Allied hands, held by a combined force of French cavalry and also V Corps of the BEF.

Fighting started south of Ypres, at La Bassée, on 10 October, and on 16 October the Allied Ypres forces began to probe out against three corps of the German Fourth Army, while the German Sixth Army was pushing forward against positions around Armentières, situated between La Bassée and Ypres itself. Then on the 18th, the combined might of the German Fourth and Sixth Armies began a thrust against Ypres, in an attempt to break through the city and secure the Channel ports to the west.

We need a sense of both the geography of the region plus the emotions behind the strategic decisions made in 1914. Ypres was in many ways a backstop for the British, and not an altogether logical one at that. During the geographical jostling of that bloody autumn, the British found themselves in position of a salient that arced out into German lines and had a perimeter of roughly 16 miles (26km). The eastern perimeter of the salient was inscribed by a series of ridges, described in military nomenclature as hills but actually gently rolling undulations, the highest of which, Hill 60, was only 197ft (60m) above sea level. Ypres itself was in the centre of the base of the salient, set on the Menin Road along which the Germans attacked in their attempt to cut out the salient and reach the coast.

During October, it appeared to many, that Ypres would fall to the German thrust. A reinforced Sixth Army made a renewed push between Messines and the Menin Road, and the next day Gheluvelt – a key village just 8 miles (13km) from the centre of Ypres – fell to the Germans. Yet this was no easy victory for the Germans. Some 1,000 British soldiers inflicted hefty losses on thirteen battalions of German troops, shattering the offensive momentum of the Germans in the process. The line had moved but was holding for the British, and such consolidation was supported by the fact that the French were also cementing their defensive lines around Ypres. The Germans summoned their strength once more, and, on 11 November, unleashed twelve and a half divisions against the Allied lines, striking between Dixmude and Messines. Despite the ferocity of the assault, and the fact that the Germans had a superiority of four divisions compared to the enemy who opposed them, the attack was blunted with devastating losses.

The French general, Joseph Joffre, later recounted the steps of the German collapse at First Ypres, while also looking ahead to the subsequent style of warfare that bedevilled the sector:

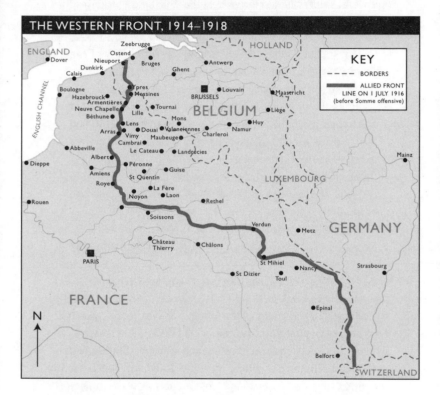

By the 14th [November] our troops had again begun to progress, barring the road to Ypres against the German attacks, and inflicting on the enemy, who advanced in massed formation, losses which were especially terrible in consequence of the fact that the French and British artillery had crowded nearly 300 guns on to these few kilometres of front.

Thus the main mass of the Germans sustained the same defeat as the detachments operating further to the north along the coast. The support which, according to the idea of the German General Staff, the attack on Ypres was to render to the coastal attack, was as futile as that attack itself had been.

During the second half of November the enemy, exhausted and having lost in the Battle of Ypres alone more than 150,000 men, did not attempt to renew his effort, but confined himself to an intermittent cannonade.

We, on the contrary, achieved appreciable progress to the north and south of Ypres, and insured definitely by a powerful defensive organization of the position the inviolability of our front.

Joseph Joffre, in *Source Records of the Great War*, Vol. II, ed. Charles F. Horne (National Alumni, 1923).

By 22 November, First Ypres had run its course. The perimeter of the salient had shrunk to 11 miles (18km), but Ypres stood safe. As with almost all calculations of the First World War battle casualties, the true cost of First Ypres will never be known. The losses were definitely heavy – an educated estimation is around 58,000 British, up to 85,000 French (reminding us of the dominant French role in First Ypres) and 21,500 Belgians. Yet German losses were almost certainly north of 100,000, likely to be around 134,000, and in the brutal calculus of attrition that dominated military thinking during the First World War, this made First Ypres an Allied victory.

Yet we have to ask, was Ypres itself worth holding? Salients are typically costly places to hold, being on the receiving end of numerous attacks and heavy artillery fire. The classic military thinking is that lines should be straightened to make them more defendable. For this, and other reasons, many military historians have questioned the value of holding the salient; such as Lyn MacDonald in her highly recommended book *Passchendaele: The Story of the Third Battle of Ypres 1917*:

> The sensible thing would have been to withdraw from the salient, abandoning Ypres, and establish a stronger line in the rear beyond the canal bank [the Ypres Canal, which ran north–south through the city], a tactical possibility which had indeed been earlier considered. But emotion was riding high, at least in Britain, where the flags waved and the drums beat and the newspapers trumpeted forth glory in every edition. Public opinion, like Queen Victoria during the Crimean War, was not interested in the possibility of defeat.
> Lyn MacDonald, *Passchendaele* (London: Penguin, 2013) p.8.

MacDonald, here speaking about the Ypres situation in 1915, sees the key reasons for holding Ypres as emotional rather than tactical – the Allies simply didn't want to see any more land fall into German hands, or the losses sustained in defending Ypres being made pointless by withdrawal. Indeed, MacDonald goes on to point out that General Sir Horace Smith-Dorrien, of the British Second Army, did indeed propose a reduction of the salient in 1915, but was removed from command for his temerity.

Yet for the all the costliness of the Ypres Salient, a case for its military merit can be made. For example, even allowing for the depth of the salient, the distance between the front line and the coastal ports was less than 18 miles (30km), and any lessening of that distance raised the future prospect of a concerted German push reaching the sea. Also, just west of Ypres were major British logistical centres, including twenty-seven railheads and seven ammunition dumps. The range of German field artillery at this time was between 6,000 and (at the extreme end) 20,000 yards (5,486m and 18,288m), so reducing the depth of the salient could have brought more vital supply bases within gun range. Shortening the salient also meant that the British and Allies would have further to cover in future offensives to reach the strategic ridgelines. The vital German railhead at Roulers lay behind the German front line, pushing arms and men into battle directly from the Ruhr. Keeping the salient meant that the British would have a better shot in the future at severing this vital communication hub.

So Ypres was not necessarily a strategic folly – whatever its status, however, it would be a costly acquisition.

The Ongoing Battle and Second Ypres

First Ypres had cost the BEF dearly. The fighting had reduced some of the British battalions to little more than an officer and fewer than 100 men. Furthermore, Ypres itself was now the subject of a steady German bombardment, which would roll on with sluggish brutality for much of the rest of the war. Ypres itself would be gutted by high-explosive, its once-beautiful medieval civic centre reduced to shattered angles and gaunt ruins.

Yet the salient, as blasted as it would become, was to be held. Manpower was required, and the encouragement of volunteerism in Britain ultimately filled the gaps. Encouraged by jingoistic newspapers, posters and cinema reels, some 2.6 million British men joined up in 1915. The recruitment was also supplemented by the ingress of soldiery from across the British Empire. Ypres received a strong contingent of Canadians plus a regiment from the Indian Army. The Canadians in particular would go on to have a ferocious and bloody relationship with Ypres.

In terms of the wider war, 1915 broke with both sides unhappy with the stalemate and looking for offensive means of breaking through the enemy's lines. The French had launched a costly and inconsequential campaign in Artois in December 1914, and this sputtered on in fits and starts until March 1915, by which time the German front line had scarcely moved and the French had lost 240,000 men.

DID YOU KNOW?

Second Ypres was not the first time poison gas had been used in the conflict. Tear gas and other irritant munitions had been applied in small quantities by the Germans at Neuve Chapelle in October 1914 and in actions in Poland in January 1915.

As winter turned to spring, the British also made an offensive move, launching a major attack at Neuve Chapelle in the Artois on 10 March. This effort was a moderate success. The initial thrust, supported by a short but stunning artillery barrage, took Neuve Chapelle in the initial assault, and broke open the German lines. Yet the casualties suffered during the first phase of the attack, and British problems in transferring reserves to the front, meant that the attack petered out within three days, the British repelling a German counter-attack but unable to push further on and secure the Aubers Ridge.

The Aubers Ridge remained an inexorable draw for the Allied commanders. Together the French and the British commanders, on 29 March 1915 at Chantilly, planned a joint offensive in the Artois, with the Aubers and Vimy Ridges as the objectives. The Germans had their own plans, which once again focused on the Ypres Salient bulging out into their lines. The German offensive, courtesy of the Fourth Army, was launched at 1700 hrs on 22 April. Its strategic objective was essentially to cut out the salient while also making some meaningful noises on the Western Front, to keep the British and French busy while Germany was heavily engaged on the Eastern Front. What made 'Second Ypres' so distinctive in the history of the war was the weapon that Germany decided to deploy to break the enemy lines – poison gas. Yet the use of lethal chemicals on the battlefield was specifically forbidden by Article 23 of the Hague Convention. Although several leading German commanders considered poison gas to be unethical or unmanly in nature, their squeamishness was overridden by General Erich von Falkenhayn, the chief of the German general staff.

The preparatory shelling of the Allied lines at Ypres began at 0500 hrs, with light field artillery hitting the front-line positions while the German heavy artillery reached into the centre of Ypres, with bloody results for the civilians there. The gas was meant to be the prelude to the infantry attack; it would be dispersed from 5,730 forward-emplaced gas cylinders, each 3ft 6in (1m) long. The problem for the Germans was that the wind was blowing in the wrong direction for much of the day, prohibiting the release of the gas until the late afternoon, when the winds changed. The valves were opened and a new, dreadful era in warfare began.

The first formations to receive the yellow-green chlorine gas were the Canadian 3rd Brigade and the French Algerian 45th Colonial Division. The effects were horrendous, both psychologically and physically. Thousands of soldiers were choking for survival, and behind the gas came wave after wave of German infantry, naturally hoping to exploit the situation they had imposed. Two French divisions collapsed, exposing the flank of the Canadian 1st Division, and the Germans also managed to secure Langemarck, Pilckem, St Julien and Gravenstafel within two days of the attack beginning. The Canadian division mounted an epic defence, stretching themselves to breaking point to cover the gap left by the retreating French divisions.

Ultimately, the British, Commonwealth and French forces could not resist the weight of the German infantry and artillery, and a general withdrawal was conducted on 1 May, back to a new line of resistance. The German offensive eventually sputtered out during May, but by 25 May the British front line around Ypres had shrunk considerably. At its deepest point, the salient was now just 2½ miles (4km) from the centre of Ypres, and well within the shelling range of most variants of German artillery. Another 58,000 Allied casualties and 38,000 German losses meant that Ypres was rapidly becoming a place of sheer human attrition.

Gas Effects

Sir Arthur Conan Doyle, then aged 55 but a signed-up infantryman nonetheless, described what he witnessed of the gas attack during Second Ypres:

> The French troops, staring over the top of the parapet at this curious screen which ensured them a temporary relief from fire, were observed to suddenly throw up their hands, to clutch at their throats, and to fall to the ground in agonies of asphyxiation. Many lay where they had fallen, while their comrades, absolutely helpless against this diabolical agency, rushed madly out of the mephitic mist and made for the rear, over-running the lines of the trenches between them. Many of them never halted until they had reached Ypres, while others rushed westwards and the put the canal between themselves and the enemy.
>
> Arthur Conan Doyle, *The British Campaign in France and Flanders 1915* (London, Hodder & Stoughton, 1919) e-book.

British gunners in gas masks, 1917. Gas was used on the Flanders front from 1915, but improved gas masks helped reduce the numbers of casualties by the time of Third Ypres.

The Build-up to Third Ypres

The strategic situation for the British at Ypres between June 1915 and June 1917 was grim. In general, the Allies in Belgium were confined to a relatively narrow strip of the country, pressed against the coast and with most of Flanders, including the coastal towns of Ostend and Zeebrugge, in German hands. Because the Germans had supply lines stretching back to Germany, and the advantages of the rail network, they were in a far stronger situation (although Flanders was not an easy logistical supply route even for the Germans – see 'The Legacy' chapter below). They took advantage of this situation by constructing a powerful network of ferro-concrete emplacements along their front lines. These were monstrous positions, capable of shrugging off even the heaviest Allied shells that smashed down onto their roofs. In these positions they sat out the war in relative protection for the next two years.

The situation over the other side of the wire was somewhat different. The Allied forces did not have the requisite supplies of concrete and other construction materials to create a substantial bunker system. Instead they hewed trenches in to the clay-heavy, sodden ground of Flanders. This land was damp and unwieldy at the best of times, but the constant German shelling had served to smash up the drainage networks that laced the land, effectively returning the countryside to the bog that it originally was. The consequences for the Allied troops were some of the most appalling living and operating conditions on the Western Front.

Strategically, the situation at Ypres in 1915 had little to recommend it for the Allies. The front line ran from just north of Nieuport, following the River Yser around Dixmude before swelling out around Ypres, then cutting back in sharply under the strategically important high ground of the Messines Ridge to the south. The land north of Ypres was largely inundated, so if the Germans wanted to press through to the coast behind Ypres the best route was to strike directly through Ypres itself. The Germans were essentially clustered around the salient, occupying the key ridgelines with their infantry and also their artillery observers, who could mercilessly direct the fire of the German big guns onto the Allied positions laid out in front of them. Just moving, letting alone fighting, was a challenge for the beleaguered Allied defenders.

The British answer to the stalemate on the Western Front was offensives, regularly conducted with the aim of breaking through the German front lines and shifting the enemy onto the back foot. And yet, between 1915 and 1917 the Ypres sector remained largely static. From June 1915 until the end of the year, the offensive activities were mostly confined (on the Western Front, at least) to Champagne and Artois, albeit with little overall change in the configuration of the front line. The following year, 1916, was dominated by two of the most destructive and prolonged battles in the history of warfare – Verdun and the Somme – both of which consumed the lives and efforts of hundreds of thousands of men, while the men of Flanders continued their stubborn and frequently monotonous stand-off with the Germans opposite.

A French villager returns home after shelling around Ypres. Many Flanders villages were virtually erased from the ground by the constant artillery bombardments.

Field Marshal Douglas Haig. He was a controversial historical figure and many blame Haig for the extreme levels of British casualties suffered at Third Ypres.

German U-boat UB14 with its crew on deck. The U-boat, as in the Second World War, was one of the greatest threats to the British war effort.

In fact, back in January 1916 the British commander-in-chief, General (later Field Marshal) Douglas Haig, had begun planning for offensives in Flanders. The Somme and Verdun had put paid to any meaningful action in Belgium in 1916, but mining operations against the Messines Ridge and other major landmarks around Ypres did begin in earnest, and continued throughout the year and into 1917. Yet the vast blood-letting of 1916 had made many in the British Establishment rather fearful of major offensive enterprises. Prime Minister David Lloyd George, was one of the most cautious individuals, and so Haig had his work cut out persuading the government to permit a Flanders campaign.

Haig was a persistent and persuasive negotiator. He argued that a Flanders campaign would not only relieve pressure from the French in the south (the French Army at this time was in a state of disarray and mutiny following the failed Nivelle Offensive) but also the Russians to the east. The further objectives of an offensive at Ypres were later spelt out (somewhat defensively) in the 1920s, by General Sir John Humphrey Davison, the Director of Military Operations at General Headquarters under Haig:

> The objects before the British in delivering the offensive in Flanders were briefly, from a strategical point of view, to pin the German Army to the British front in the North and draw in their Reserves; and from a tactical point of view:
> (a) To free Ypres by gaining the Passchendaele ridge which lies in a semi-circle round the eastern side and dominates the town and surrounding country.
> (b) To gain the Passchendaele ridge, thereby commanding with long-range gunfire the enemy's communications through Roulers and his submarine bases at Ostend and Zeebrugge.
> (c) To exploit to the full any tactical success gained (for this special preparations were made).
> Humphrey Davison, in *Source Records of the Great War*, Vol. V, ed. Charles F. Horne (National Alumni, 1923), quoted in www. firstworldwar.com.

The second point in Davison's argument is critical. Haig at first met with a wall of near-hostility to his plans for a Flanders offensive, not just from Lloyd George but also from many others in the cabinet, and even from members of the military high command. At a meeting on 17 June 1917, Haig's confident predictions for a Flanders offensive were pushed back at him across the table, and his subsequent arguments weren't helped by the recent Somme experience.

Yet a change was coming. Haig was suddenly aided by the opinions of the First Sea Lord, Admiral Jellicoe, who stated to the government that the maritime losses from the German unrestricted submarine campaign were reaching unsustainable levels. On this basis, it was critical that Ostend and Zeebrugge were brought back into Allied hands without delay. The urgency of time also countered another argument brought against Haig's plans. The United States had joined the war on 6 April 1917, and the defensive 'hold fast' strategy was based on Lloyd George's hopes that the American contribution would finally tip the war in their favour. However, the build-up of US troops to meaningful levels was going to take many more months, and according to Jellicoe those months were not available.

Haig's arguments now found more receptive ears, aided by the successful operation against the Messines Ridge between 7 and 14 June (see next chapter for details). By 21 June he was authorised to push on with preparations for a Flanders offensive, and discussions were to open with the French about what levels of support they could provide for the operation. Davison clarifies the outcome of these discussions:

DID YOU KNOW?

In 1915, the German U-boats sank a total of 1.3 million tonnes of Allied shipping. In 1917, by contrast, that figure rose to a total of 6.2 million tonnes.

In order to gain strength for offensive purposes and to increase the number of our available reserves we had entered into negotiations with the French to take over part of our defensive front. This, however, they were unwilling to do, but requested to be allowed to take a small part in the Flanders offensive. It was considered advisable to acquiesce in their demands, but this was done with great reluctance and disappointment, for the mixture of French, Belgian and British troops in a confined area was not conducive to success, and their infantry, guns and ammunition arrived late, thereby delaying the commencement of operations until the 31st of July and involving the loss of many days of valuable summer weather which would have been of incalculable advantage in view of the exceptionally bad weather experienced in August.

Humphrey Davison, in Horne, *Source Records*.

As we see here, Davison views the French participation in the Battle of Ypres as more of a hindrance than a help. Nevertheless, the momentum towards a Ypres offensive was now inexorable.

THE ARMIES

The First World War tends to have a bad press when it comes to military innovation. Popular depictions of the war tend to focus on ranks of doomed men walking stoically into rattling machine-gun fire, with generals far behind the front lines casually ordering them to their deaths. Thankfully, careful research has progressively dispelled many over simplifications. Viewed with a more circumspect eye, the First World War helped develop some of the tactics and technologies that inform warfare to this day. Innovations included: the development of precision artillery barrages and fire-control techniques; armoured vehicles; combat aircraft (fighters, bombers and reconnaissance aircraft); submarines; flamethrowers; raiding tactics; machine-gun fire control; the construction of ferro-concrete field fortifications; early military radio communications; and more effective front-line logistics. There were, of course, many instances of retrograde tactical thinking, but we should never overlook the advances that were made by more thoughtful tacticians and engineers.

In this chapter, we will take a look at the Allied and Axis armies of mid-1917, examining where they were in terms of tactical outlook, fighting efficiency and technology. The picture is a mixed one. On one level, as we shall see, many units were still mud-drenched foot-sloggers, fighting their war with solid but basic arms. From a different angle, however, we see armies with new professional skills, particularly in the harnessing of explosive firepower. The two sides of the coin go a long way to explaining the horror of what occurred at Passchendaele.

The British and Commonwealth Forces

The aforementioned General Davison, writing in the 1920s, had few illusions about the experience of the soldiery at Passchendaele. He described their suffering there with pained eloquence:

> The word 'Passchendaele' was and has been used as a reproach to British generalship, and as a symbol of waste and useless suffering.
>
> To the men who actually fought, such an attitude might be intelligible, for their horizon was limited by the expanse of mud and waste on every hand, by the incessant fire to which they were subjected, by the comparatively insignificant gains of ground at great sacrifice, and by the abnormal fatigue and hardship.
>
> Similarly to the wounded and to those who had lost their husbands, sons and brothers it appeared that heavy suffering had been inflicted and limbs and lives lost with little or no result so far as winning the war was concerned.
>
> To the gunner during the latter period of the offensive, day in and day out handling his mud-spattered ammunition with unspeakable fatigue, constantly endeavouring to save his guns from disappearing into the morass, serving his pieces clustered round the only solid means of approach, the duckboard pathway, under a concentrated and almost continuous hail of enemy projectiles; to the infantryman heavily equipped staggering through an interminable sea of mud towards what appeared to him as certain death, the physical and mental strain was well-nigh unbearable. A blank wall on every side and no apparent end to the misery.
>
> Humphrey Davison, in Horne, *Source Records.*

From a leading member of the high command during the Great War, this depiction is notably frank. It shows a soldiery struggling against the timeless challenges of mud, fatigue, fear and disorientation, with just their physical survival the foremost priority in their minds. Using this picture as context, there is little doubt that the Battle of Passchendaele was, for the men who fought it, a physically basic affair. Yet the British Army of 1917 was, in many ways, different to that of 1914, both structurally and psychologically.

Structure

As we have already noted, the British Army in the first two years of the war was filled by the soldiers of the regular army and the legions of enthusiastic volunteers who joined up in 1915. Conscription, however, was introduced in May 1916. The primary aim of this policy was not necessarily to draw ever greater numbers of men into the ranks of the military, but to regulate the numbers of men kept in manufacturing, mining and other essential war work back in the UK. The relatively efficient handling of recruitment into the services meant that the British Army would find itself well supplied with military manpower. However, the massive ingress of men was essential, especially once major campaigns such as the Somme stripped out tens of thousands of men from the ranks.

DID YOU KNOW?

The First World War meant that almost an entire generation experienced military service. By the end of the war 5.7 million men were in uniform as opposed to the 733,000 on mobilisation in 1914.

The individual British 'Tommy' would find himself placed within the layered structure of the British Army. The heart of the British organisational structure was the infantry division, two to six of which would be assigned to a corps, and two or more corps to an army. In terms of its foot soldiers, the infantry division was organised into three infantry brigades, each of four infantry battalions. (Note that each battalion belonged to a particular infantry regiment, but the battalions of that regiment would typically be split between different divisions.) The rule of four continued downwards – each battalion consisted of four infantry companies, and each company of four platoons. The total strength of a division, on paper at least, was around 10,000–12,000 men.

Yet the divisional strength was not just a matter of infantrymen. By 1917 the division had grown into a sprawling network of combat, communications and logistical specialities. By April 1917, for example, a division had four machine-gun companies to its credit, with each company having some sixteen Vickers heavy machine guns (HMGs), apart from the divisional machine-gun company which had four HMGs. (Battalion machine-gun firepower was provided through the liberal volumes of Lewis light machine guns increasingly added to the division throughout the war.)

Heavier firepower was also provided by the divisional artillery, manned by nearly 3,000 men and with logistics supplied by 280 vehicles and more than 2,000 horses, the latter reminding us that mechanisation of the military forces was still very much in its infancy. The divisional artillery in 1917 consisted of two field artillery brigades, each of three field-gun batteries and a field howitzer battery. Each field-gun battery provided medium-range fire support via 6 x 18pdr guns, while the field howitzer battery delivered thunderous destruction from 6 x 4.5in howitzers.

Apart from the field artillery brigades, the other important strand of the divisional artillery was the trench mortar brigade, increasingly useful in an age where delivering indirect trench-to-trench fire was essential. The brigade was structured around three medium batteries (each of 4 x 4in mortars) and a heavy battery (4 x 9.45in mortars).

Moving away from the combat elements, the infantry division depended on massive logistical support to keep working and fighting. There were three field companies of Royal Engineers, performing all manner of battlefield and rear-area engineering challenges, while a signals company had the frequently thankless and often lethal task of trying to keep communications flowing between front-line units and headquarters or other command posts. Medical emergencies were handled by the Royal Army Medical Corps, which had three field ambulance companies and a sanitary section (the duties of the latter, primarily focused on preventing disease, were sorely tested in the thoroughly insanitary conditions of Passchendaele).

From 1916, each division also included a pioneer battalion (an entire Labour Corps was eventually formed in 1917), of around 1,000 men plus twelve Lewis guns for fire support. Divisional labourers were, in many senses, every bit as much combatants as those responsible for assaulting enemy trenches. Here Corporal J.C. Morgan, a member of a labour company at Passchendaele, defends his profession:

The delusion existed, and probably still exists, that no labour companies were ever nearer the line than twenty miles. But when I tell you that the company to which I belonged – originally half of a Scottish labour battalion – was for the last seventeen months of the War never at any moment out of range of Jerry's guns, and that when he did get us he got us with his biggest guns and with his high-velocities, from which there was no dodging, and that during the struggle for Passchendaele in the autumn of 1917 our company were awarded a Military Cross, a DCM, and eight MM's – well, we must have been within hearing distance, anyway.

The word 'labour' also gave people the impression that we were an uneducated, uncivilised, unwashed lot of beings, whereas we were composed of exactly the same sort of men as every other branch of the service, except that most of us were

short-sighted, and some of us wanted a finger, or possessed
varicose veins, or suffered from some other stroke of luck.

Corporal J.C. Morgan in *Everyman at War*, ed. C.B. Purdom
(London: J.M. Dent, 1939), quoted in www.firstworldwar.com.

Morgan makes the point, to which we shall explicitly and implicitly
return throughout this book, that the long-range attrition of
artillery meant that very few soldiers were truly out of harm's way.
This also applied to the divisional train – around 180 vehicles and
400 horses – which had to haul divisional supplies to and from the
front line on roads generally zeroed by the enemy guns.

Thus we have a general picture of the British Army division.
Yet to this picture we must add the contribution made by the
Commonwealth. We should never forget that the 'British' Army
was in many ways an international force. In January 1917, of eighty-
nine British divisions in France and Flanders, a total of nineteen
were either Indian or Commonwealth forces. At Third Ypres, the
Australians, New Zealanders and Canadians made inestimable
and bloody sacrifices on the battlefield. The Australian and New
Zealand Army Corps (ANZACs) cumulatively contributed nearly
500,000 men to the war effort, and lost thousands of men at Third
Ypres. The Canadian Corps added 24,132 men to the front line,
and they also threw their all into the Third Battle of Ypres, when
the Canadian Corps relieved the II ANZAC Corps during the Second
Battle of Passchendaele in late October 1917. Canadian and ANZAC
divisions followed the British Army's divisional structure.

Command

At the top of the command tree for the British forces in 1917 was
Field Marshal Douglas Haig, commander of the BEF. Such is the
controversy that surrounds this figure in history, that it is often
difficult to separate the fact from the fiction. In the post-war years,
thanks to a combination of David Lloyd George's memoirs and a
growing public revulsion at the casualties of the First World War,

he came to epitomise a form of callous generalship that consigned hundreds of thousands of men to untimely and brutal deaths, often for scant physical advance. Above all, he is regarded as one of the 'donkeys' leading the 'lions'.

More recent biographies of Haig paint, if not a favourable picture of the man, then at least a more balanced one. Haig could visibly appear gruff and dismissive on emotional topics, but some of this was partly due to his lack of trust in politicians and journalists. He certainly presided over some of the greatest bloodbaths in British military history – none more so than the Somme and Third Ypres – which seem to be profound expressions of military futility. Yet to be fair to Haig, and to many commanders of the First World War, they were faced by one of the more challenging strategic situations any military leader could face. Strongly entrenched front-line positions, with no flanks to turn, meant that there were few options for the assault other than bludgeoning frontal attacks, supported by artillery and other firepower.

The questions surrounding his handling of battles such as the Somme and Third Ypres, however, often revolve around the duration of time over which he sustained operations, not necessarily over whether the offensive action itself was right. In addition, we must remember that Haig also presided over the great British victories of 1918, which are discussed far less often than the terrible battles of 1916 and 1917. Such is not to say that Haig's reputation should be entirely restored, but we should recognise that the elements in arguing over his reputation are more nuanced than often credited.

The major British formations involved in the Battle of Passchendaele were the Fifth Army and, supporting to the south, the Second Army. Between them they brought the following corps to the battlefield:

Second Army
IX Corps
X Corps

I ANZAC Corps
II ANZAC Corps
Canadian Corps

Fifth Army
II Corps
XIV Corps
XVIII Corps
XIX Corps

The Second Army was led by Field Marshal Herbert Plumer, who was a true soldier's commander. Having joined the 65th Foot in 1876, he rose through the ranks of the army quickly on the basis of merit rather than social influence, cutting his operational teeth in the conflicts in South Africa during the late 1800s and early 1900s. Plumer was in charge of the Second Army from May 1915, helping to save the salient for the British, and still held that command during the critical offensive years of 1917 and 1918.

Field Marshal Herbert Plumer was a highly competent and resourceful commander of the British Second Army. He virtually took over the Third Ypres campaign from Gough in August 1917.

He was known by the men as 'Old Plum and Apple' or 'Daddy Plumer', and exhibited that balanced combination of humour, humanity and discipline that won both the respect and the favour of the troops under his command.

The respect of the soldiers under one's command does not automatically equate with the respect of one's superiors and peers. Haig never entirely warmed to the cautious and circumspect Plumer, and nor did Plumer see eye-to-eye with the Fifth Army's commander, Hubert Gough. Yet in many ways Plumer was one of Haig's more competent commanders. Not only did Plumer preside over the resounding success of the Messines Ridge attack in early July 1917, he was also subsequently used to try to restore the offensive at Ypres, when Gough's efforts had stalled. Later he led successful operations on the Italian Front in the winter of 1917, and on the Western Front in 1918.

Alongside Plumer at Passchendaele was Sir Hubert Gough, commander of the Fifth Army. Gough was a very different character to Plumer, and had built his reputation as a forceful cavalry commander. Yet unlike Plumer, Gough's reputation would be undermined by the Battle of Passchendaele, not cemented by it. Following his replacement by General Sir William Birdwood in 1918, he did not attain a major command position for the rest of the war.

General Sir Hubert Gough (1870–1963)

General Sir Hubert Gough was born into a family of glittering military pedigree – his father, uncle and brother were all Victoria Cross winners. The young Gough went on to join the 16th Lancers in 1889, and as a courageous cavalryman he steadily rose through the ranks of the British Army, being appointed commander of the 16th Lancers in 1907. Gough also weathered a political storm in 1914, when, as commander of 3rd Cavalry Brigade, he led a group of British officers who refused to conduct operations against Ulster loyalists in Northern Ireland. Despite his place in the 'Curragh Mutiny', Gough's career did not suffer appreciably. He fought during the battles of manoeuvre in 1914, being appointed to command the 14th Cavalry Division in September before leading the 7th Division from April 1915 and ICorp from the following July. Gough struck up close connections with Haig, who appreciated the fellow cavalryman's aggressive outlook. He took over the British Reserve Army in May 1916, which (following its supporting role in the Battle of the Somme) was renamed the Fifth Army. It was this formation, with Gough at the helm, that led the way at Third Ypres, although the lack of breakthrough plus heavy losses compelled Haig to shift the weight of the offensive to Plumer's Second Army. Worse was to come. In March 1918, Gough was blamed for the collapse of the Fifth Army in the face of the German spring offensive, and was dismissed from his command. The dismissal was as much for political as for military reasons, but the only further command Gough held was chief of the Allied Mission to the Baltic, between 1919 and 1922.

General Sir Hubert Gough had his reputation as a commander severely dented by the Third Ypres campaign, his costly tactics buying few gains on the ground.

General Friedrich Bertram Sixt von Armin (1851–1936)

While Third Ypres was the low point in the careers for many Allied commanders, for Friedrich von Arnim, commander of the German Fourth Army, the battle brought him decorations and acknowledgements. At the age of 19 he joined the 4th Grenadier Guards regiment, experiencing combat and wounds during the Franco-Prussian War. His bravery in that war saw him awarded the Iron Cross, Second Class, and he also began a steady rise through the ranks, occupying both field and staff positions (the latter included Director of the General Department of War in the Prussian War Ministry in 1903). By 1900 he was an Oberst commanding a regiment, and divisional (1908) and corps (1911) commands came in regular order. Von Arnim was a competent and professionally successful commander who understood the principles of both attack and defence. His handling of IX Corps during the early years of the war, including in major clashes such as the Somme, brought him the award of the Pour le Mérite. Equally, his handling of a tenacious defence at Third Ypres (he took over command of the Fourth Army on 25 February 1917) saw further decorations – the Order of the Black Eagle, plus the oak leaf cluster to the Pour le Mérite. Von Arnim led the Fourth Army through to the end of the war, finally resigned from military service in 1919 following general demobilisation.

General Friedrich von Arnim was the commander of the German Fourth Army, which capably defended against the British offensive in Flanders in 1917.

The French Army

Although the Battle of Passchendaele is often treated as a largely British affair, we must also recognise the important role of French forces in the battle, particularly the efforts of six divisions of the French First Army under the command of General Francoise Paul Anthoine. The First Army was a wartime creation, mobilised in August 1914 to face the threat of German forces sweeping down from Belgium. By the time it reached 1917, it was a war-weary unit, having suffered the depredations of repeated offensives, the grim attrition of holding the line, plus the collapse in morale that followed the disastrous Nivelle Offensive (otherwise known as the Aisne Campaign) of spring 1917. As such, the French were a distinctly weakened force by the later years of the war, both physically and spiritually.

The French Army, like the British, was founded on its infantry divisions. Structurally, the French infantry division was composed of three or four infantry regiments (the French were transitioning to three-regiment divisions throughout 1917 and into 1918). Each regiment had three infantry battalions, and each battalion three infantry companies, each company in turn divided into four platoons. Battalion support came from a machine-gun company, while the companies could draw on the resources of a trench artillery platoon (3 x 37mm guns) and a machine-gun section of three or four light machine guns. The infantry had a more mobile counterpart in one or two cavalry squadrons.

The artillery component of the French division was an artillery regiment, of three field artillery batteries (each 4 x 75mm fast-firing guns) and field howitzer battery (4 x 155mm howitzers) plus a trench artillery battery and a mortar company. Divisional engineers provided two mining companies, a field part company and a signals section, while a medical section tackled the challenge of the huge number of casualties of war.

DID YOU KNOW?

The French 75mm Mle 1897 field gun was one of the best artillery pieces of the early twentieth century. It could fire continuously and accurately at rates of 15rpm and to ranges of 7,500 yards (6,858m).

Command of the French First Army, as noted, fell upon the shoulders of Francoise Anthoine. Born in 1860, Anthoine was commissioned as a lieutenant in the artillery in 1883, subsequently serving in Africa and French Indochina. He was a regimental commander by 1910, and the following year became the assistant to the deputy chief of staff of the French Army, General Noël de Castelnau. By the outbreak of the First World War, Anthoine had ascended to chief of staff of the Second Army, but in October 1914 he took the first of several combat commands, initially of the 20th Infantry Division. His leadership in battle brought him recognition and promotion, taking over X Corps in June 1915, and the Fourth Army in March 1917. He was subsequently transferred to the First Army in June 1917, and his performance in First Ypres seemed to do nothing but consolidate his reputation as a dependable and thoughtful leader of men in war. He also managed to cooperate successfully with the large personalities of the British military leadership, despite not being a huge fan of the British in general.

Following Passchendaele, Anthoine was far less successful at negotiating the politics of high command. He became chief of staff to General Philippe Pétain (the French commander-in-chief) in December 1917, but poor cooperation between the Allies oiled the wheels of German successes in the offensives of spring 1918, and Anthoine also became tarnished with accusations of poor leadership, and was replaced in July 1918. Despite this rather ignominious end to his wartime career, Anthoine certainly made a valued contribution to the Allied effort at Ypres.

The ranks for the French Army had, by 1917, been horribly decimated on the battlefields of its homeland. By early 1917 nearly one in twenty of all French males had been killed in action, a statistic that more than contextualises the mutinous events following the Nivelle Offensive. (During this turbulent period, some 43 per cent of all French infantry divisions experienced some measure of mutiny.) Pétain's subsequent reforms, however, had managed to raise the morale of the French soldiers to a functional level. Thus, the First Army that fought at Passchendaele was a mixture, as with most French armies, of grizzled and jaded veterans and youthful and fearful replacements. This being said, the French soldier continued to exhibit remarkable resilience and tenacity when required, and they should never be regarded as a second-rate partner to the British forces.

The German Army

Facing the British across the blasted Ypres Salient was the German Fourth Army, commanded by the resolute General der Infanterie Friedrich von Arnim. The Fourth Army, like the opposing Allied formations, was a veteran army by 1917. It had been mobilised in August 1914, and provided one of the principal thrusts through Belgium and Luxembourg into northern France. Its original plan of capturing Paris, however, was not fulfilled and instead it became squeezed into Flanders during the Race to the Sea. It became a permanent feature wrapped around the Ypres Salient, etching itself firmly with trenches, strongpoints, bunkers and emplacements (although in many areas it was not possible to dig trenches because of the high water table), enduring months of poor weather and regular shellfire.

The Fourth Army, prior to the Third Ypres, was divided into three major groups, which were essentially of corps strength. These were the Dixmude (XIV Corps), Ypres (III Bavarian Corps) and Wytschaete (IX Reserve Corps), between them boasting seventeen divisions. In terms of structure, the German infantry division

The blasted landscape around Ypres. Note the interlaced frames of sticks in the trenches, which acting as revetting.

of 1917 had a single infantry brigade containing three infantry regiments, each subdivided into three infantry battalions, and those into four infantry companies.

Machine-gun and mortar companies provided immediate front-line support fire, while the heavier stuff came from the division's field artillery regiment, consisting of two field gun detachments (of three batteries, each of 40 x 77mm guns) and a field howitzer detachment (40 x 105mm howitzers). From 1917 the division also had a pioneer battalion, reflecting the defensive outlook that now characterised German policy on the Western Front, which was composed of two field companies, a mortar company plus a searchlight detachment of three to six searchlights.

Other elements to the division include a cavalry squadron (which by this time was frequently used purely for manning observation posts), a 'Machine-Gun Marksmen Detachment' of around twelve heavy machine guns, a field replenishment depot and field hospital.

The towering figure over the German Army in 1917 was General Erich Ludendorff. In fact, Ludendorff was not the overall commander of the German forces – that fell to Field Marshall Paul von Hindenburg, the Imperial Army's chief of staff for whom Ludendorff served as quartermaster general, with the rank of 'General der Infanterie'. Yet in reality, it was Ludendorff who was the motive force behind German strategic policy for the much of the war, even though Hindenburg occasionally grabbed the limelight.

Ludendorff was an individual of enormous drive and self-belief, a man who had delivered major victories on both the Eastern and Western Fronts. Ludendorff was largely responsible for the intelligent adaptation of defensive tactics on the Western Front from 1917, tactics that would produce the human grinding mill experienced by British at Third Ypres. The combination of sound defensive tactics, three years of combat experience, capable

commanders and good equipment made the Fourth Army at Ypres an opponent that warranted permanent respect.

General Erich Ludendorff was one of the driving strategic thinkers of Germany's war effort between 1914 and 1918, on both Eastern and Western Fronts.

Kit and Equipment

Compared to the uniforms worn by the soldiers of today, those of the First World War were crude in the extreme. The basic British infantry uniform was the 1902 Pattern Service Dress. This was a khaki tunic and trousers, the former featuring four button-down patch pockets, an internal pocket under the tunic flap and a turned-down collar, all accented by brass buttons that needed rigorous polishing to keep clean at the front. The trousers ran down close to the leg and terminated in long woollen puttees that wrapped up from the ankle to the knee.

Footwear consisted of the B5 ammunition boots, solid leather footwear with metal-studded soles. For warmth, the soldiers could wear either an army greatcoat or the rather outlandish-looking sleeveless goatskin jerkin. The practicality of the latter was steadily undermined as the war went on; once soaked and impregnated with mud (of which there was plenty at Ypres), the jerkin lost almost all of its insulating properties, and provided a suitable breeding ground for the lice that bedevilled the soldiers' wellbeing. To protect against the abundant rainfall, the soldiers could draw upon a rubberised gas cape; during gas attacks, if the soldier was caught without a gas mask, the cape could be thrown over the head to provide a light barrier against the poisonous fumes.

In terms of protective gear, the British Tommy of the First World War relied on two main items. The first was that great identifier of the British soldier – the helmet, steel, Mk I. Prior to the introduction of the Mk I helmet in 1916, the British soldier was inadequately served by varieties of soft utility caps. Bullets and shell splinters soon revealed that these caps had no place in the modern battlefield, and John Leopold Brodie's 1.3lb (0.6kg) steel helmet resulted in a dramatic reduction in the numbers of serious head injuries.

Of equal importance to the steel helmet was the Small Box Respirator (SBR), the standard-issue gas mask for the British soldier.

It was introduced in 1916, and its waterproof mask provided full face protection from dangerous gases. Breathing was performed directly through a tube that ran into a tin cylinder ventilator box filled with gas-neutralising chemicals. It was basic protection, but it undoubtedly saved the lives of tens of thousands of Allied soldiers of the Western Front.

Looking to the French, by 1917 the ostentation of early-war French military uniforms had largely drained away from the French Army. In 1914, the uniform was a statement of bravado and pride – a red kepi pillbox hat, blue frock coat and highly visible red pantaloons. For reasons of both practicality (being visually conspicuous was an open invitation to getting shot) and production (millions of men were suddenly being thrust into uniform), the uniform was rapidly simplified to the famous 'horizon blue' tunic and trousers – a muted light-blue uniform that, when wearied with age and mud, did a respectable job of blending the soldier in with his battlefield backdrop.

It should also be noted that the French beat the British to introducing the steel helmet on the battlefield. The Adrian helmet, albeit with rather colonial contours, was first worn in the spring of 1915, and, like the Brodie helmet, played its part in lowering the rates of head injuries (although these rates stayed hideously high during the conflict).

The German Army soldier's uniform also went through several stages of rationalisation during the war. By 1917 he was wearing the all-arms *Bluse* campaign tunic and the M1916 *Stahlhelm* (steel helmet), a nickel-steel helmet that provided excellent protection to skull and neck. (Gone was the old boiled-leather spiked *Pickelhaube* helmet.) A convenient and comfortable *Sturmgepäck* (assault pack) had been developed to carry essential gear, albeit still alongside the traditional M1887 haversack. The M1907 greatcoat provided outer warmth in cold conditions. Although the quality of the German soldier's uniform became rather poor in the later years of the war, once material shortages bit into the domestic economy, he remained as well equipped as his foes.

The British Soldier

It is extremely difficult to generalise about the British Tommy of 1917. Conscription had altered the nature of the army greatly since the volunteer-fuelled army of 1914, when many battalions and regiments had been created with a definite local or regional identity. These identities persisted, but were somewhat diluted owing to the distribution of men through conscription. The ranks of the British Army represented a true cross-section of society. Much of the rank-and-file came from the urban working classes, but the professional middle classes also made up a significant proportion of both enlisted men and battlefield officers. (The upper classes had provided much of the officer class in the early years of the war, but their ranks had been thinned and positions opened by the terrible losses of 1914–16.) In essence, the British soldier of 1917 belonged to a less stratified organisation, what military historian John Terraine classifies as a true 'Citizen Army'. Each soldier went through around two months of basic training in the UK before being posted overseas, and if assigned to the combat infantry would eventually take up one of four roles in a twelve-man section: a 'bomber' (deploying hard grenades), 'rifleman', 'Lewis gunner' or 'rifle grenadier' (skilled in using rifle-launched grenades). His section, platoon and company became his world, and his sector of front his physical horizon. Frequently cynical, and given to express his views through a black and mocking humour (expressed most perfectly in front-line newspapers such as the *Wipers Times*), the British soldier was nevertheless capable of the most extraordinary endurance and also patriotism. During the war itself, the modern world-weary disillusion with the aims of the Great War would have often found rebuttal amongst the ranks of even the most battle-scarred veterans.

The German Soldier

The German soldier of 1917 was a valued commodity. Manpower shortages in the German Army had forced Hindenburg and Ludendorff to implement the 'Hindenburg Programme' in 1916, designed both to increase armed forces manpower and munitions and weapons output to required levels. Thus Germany's reserve manpower was combed for front-line soldiers, but at the same time many tens of thousands of troops were sent home to resume careers in specialist engineering. Ludendorff hoped that in many ways future manpower limitations would be offset by the larger volumes of automatic weaponry and artillery. By consequence, many of the German Fourth Army units of 1917 were a mix of dwindling numbers of veterans set against a backdrop of very young recruits (17–20 years old) and troops combed out from either reserve formations or other divisions deployed elsewhere in the German theatres. Training times for the new soldier were short, often just 1–3 months back in Germany and 2–3 weeks at a field recruit depot just behind the front line. (The large numbers of machine guns in the German Army was in some measure a compensation for poor general training in rifle skills amongst the infantry.) The recruit depots were often composed of soldiers from the same locality back in Germany (the location of their home depot), but once training was complete they tended to be distributed throughout the wider army, not just to their attached division. This resulted in the scattering of local friendships, but it also had the effect of minimising losses for one particular village or town back in Germany.

Weapons

The First World War sits at a transitional time in the history of warfare. Rifled breech-loading artillery and firearms had only established themselves fully in the arsenals of international armies in the second half of the nineteenth century. In many ways, therefore, the full potential for destruction of these weapons had yet to be experienced by many of the world's armies (although the international navies were under fewer illusions). In an age that still lauded the heroism and spirit of the individual warrior, the fact that 70 per cent of all casualties would be inflicted by artillery batteries, hundreds of yards behind the front line, was a difficult lesson to take. Furthermore, three men operating an HMG could inflict the casualties of a platoon of riflemen, as long as the team kept the weapon levelled at the attackers, cooled or changed its barrels periodically and had a ready supply of ammunition.

The lessons were progressively absorbed by all sides in the conflict, as we shall observe below. However, the fact remains that in denuded landscapes with no flanks, the new weapons of warfare were in ideal conditions to show their full scope for destruction.

Small Arms and Machine Guns

Although they were basic compared to today's automatic weapons, we mustn't underestimate the power and utility of the bolt-action rifles. The British/Commonwealth soldier had the .303in Short Magazine Lee Enfield (SMLE); the German the 7.92mm Mauser Gewehr 98; the French the 8mm Mle 1886 Lebel or one of several variants of 8mm Berthier rifles. Each had its own advantages and disadvantages, but the basic proposition of what these weapons offered was the same.

All these weapons were capable of accurate shots over many hundreds of yards; with an optical scope, the Mauser and SMLE in particular were viable sniper weapons out to 1,000 yards (914m).

DID YOU KNOW?

The British SMLE rifle had the advantage of the largest magazine capacity – ten rounds – compared to the five-round box of the German Mauser and the five to eight rounds held in French rifle magazines.

For this reason, the threat from snipers was a very real one for all those occupying front-line trenches. Exposing just a sliver of skull above the parapet was likely to bring an immediate and generally fatal head wound; dips in the trench parapet were well signposted, reminding the wandering soldier to duck as he passed them.

Yet, as well as precision weapons, the rifles of the day were also capable of delivering heavy firepower, especially from the barrels of a coordinated defence. For a trained infantryman, fifteen aimed shots a minute were possible by virtue of the combination of magazine feed and a smooth bolt action. During the early battles of 1914, especially at Mons, there were occasions when the Germans faced such intense rippling rifle fire that they presumed their opponents were armed with machine guns.

The soldiers at Third Ypres carried other personal weapons. The officers in particular had a variety of handguns. The British almost exclusively used service revolvers made by the Webley Company, these offered a man-stopping blow via hefty .455in-calibre rounds, fed from a six-round cylinder. The recoil of this weapon, however, meant that the Webley revolvers were brutes to handle, unlike the German semi-automatic offerings. The short-recoil operated 7.63mm Mauser 'Broomhandle' gun may have looked awkward, but it handled smoothly and accurately, and had the advantage of a ten-round integral magazine.

Alternatively, the German officer could opt for the 9mm Parabellum Model 1908 'Luger', a weapon of such quality that it

DID YOU KNOW?

All armies were issued with unnerving bayonets as standard during the First World War. Yet despite training investment in bayonet fighting, most research has revealed that the bayonet was rarely used in combat itself, and found itself more readily applied as a utility tool. In fact, only 0.32 per cent of combat wounds in the First World War were attributed to bayonets.

would serve the German Army effectively for nearly half a century. The French officer would typically have a Mle 1892 'Lebel' pistol, another revolver. Unlike the British .455in cartridge, however, the Mle 1892 fired a rather weak 8mm cartridge, with a muzzle velocity of just 208m/sec. For the common soldier, pistols were a rarity. In true close-range combat, therefore, he would use whatever was to hand, resulting in a fairly barbaric array of spiked clubs, knuckledusters, knives and daggers, sharpened spades and whatever else could be used to split open an enemy soldier in the confines of a trench action.

While rifles and pistols snatched away thousands of lives on the Western Front, by far the most destructive firearm was of course the machine gun. Although the belt-fed machine gun was still a relatively new phenomenon in 1914 – Hiram Maxim had pioneered his designs in the 1880s – the type had reached a level of design that ensured its scything influence over the battlegrounds of Passchendaele and other regions.

The British .303in Vickers and the German 7.92mm MG08 were both of the Maxim stable, being water-cooled, tripod-mounted, belt-fed and recoil-operated guns with a cyclical rate of fire of around 450rpm. (The French Hotchkiss machine guns were somewhat different, being air cooled and fed from twenty-four- or third-round rigid metallic strips, a less satisfying alternative to the belt-fed weapons.) Kept fed with ammunition from a well-trained team, both of these machine guns could exert a terrifying command over the battlefield. Serried ranks of infantry could be chopped down in a single traverse, and an infantry squad bunched together could be dispatched in seconds. When not firing at 'point' targets, such as individuals or positions, machine guns could deliver indirect fire over several thousand yards, suppressing area targets such as rear-area troop concentrations or supply routes. Logically positioned, with interlocking fields of fire, machine guns could quite effectively dictate the outcome of an entire battle.

During the First World War, the influence of the machine gun meant that the type began to diversify into variants. While the Vickers, Maxim and Hotchkiss came to occupy the category of 'heavy machine gun' (HMG), other weapons were designed for the 'light machine gun' (LMG) role. LMGs were meant to offer the machine-gun's firepower in a more portable form, allowing the infantry assault units to take their own support fire forward

German soldiers engage a French attack on the Western Front, using precise rifle fire to pick off the attackers.

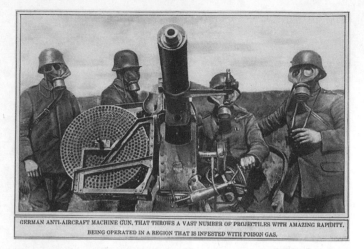

GERMAN ANTI-AIRCRAFT MACHINE GUN, THAT THROWS A VAST NUMBER OF PROJECTILES WITH AMAZING RAPIDITY, BEING OPERATED IN A REGION THAT IS INFESTED WITH POISON GAS.

German gunners man a heavy-calibre anti-aircraft machine gun, fitted with a large-capacity drum magazine.

with them. The most successful of these LMGs was the American-designed Lewis machine gun, adopted most enthusiastically by the British forces. The Lewis was not a perfect LMG by any means – it still weighed 26lb (11.8kg) and it often experienced stoppages – but it nevertheless souped-up the front-line firepower of the British Army considerably, outnumbering the Vickers by a ratio of 3:1.

German and French attempts to find a convenient SMG were less successful. The Germans simply attempted to scale down the MG08 by fitting it with a shoulder stock, pistol grip and bipod. The weight savings of the MG08/15 were actually minimal, and the weapon remained a brute to haul around the battlefield, although once it was set up and firing there was no doubting its destructive capabilities. The French had the truly terrible 8 x 50R Chauchat, a weapon that failed in terms of design, reliability and utility at almost every level.

Whatever the qualities of the First World War machine guns, the fact remained that they succeeded in filling the air of Europe with lethal hails of lead, and in the process stripped the Continent of millions of its youth.

Artillery

The First World War was undeniably an artillery war. Artillery was the primary means of inflicting attrition on the enemy – some 70 per cent of all casualties in the conflict were caused by shellfire – regardless of whether one side or the other was conducting a purposeful offensive operation. On the Western Front in particular, artillery had the reach and indirect-fire trajectory to strike along the full depth of enemy trench systems and out into rear-area supply routes, hampering the flow of logistics to the front while also limiting movement and inflicting casualties on those in front line and support positions.

In terms of types, artillery on all sides had a spectrum, from light trench-deployed pieces with a range of a few hundred yards, through to monstrous howitzers pumping out shells across many miles of distance. An entire book could be devoted to description of these, but some examples from the British Army are representative.

At the smallest end of the scale were the trench mortars. Although the Germans began the First World War with these weapons already integrated into their tactics and their arsenals, the British were slow to catch on, and in 1914–1915 introduced a hotchpotch of improvised weapons. Yet in 1915, the 3in Stokes mortar was adopted, named after its inventor, Wilfred Stokes. As a weapon against pinpoint enemy positions and trenches, the Stokes was superb. Its high arcing trajectory not only meant that it could be operated safely from the bottom of a trench, but also that the shells would drop nearly vertically into an opposing trench or bunker. A high rate of fire could be maintained – up to twenty-two bombs per minute in the hands of the trained crew – and the range was a useful 1,200 yards (1,097m). The 3in mortar quickly became an established tool for both the British and the French (the French Army borrowed the design) and it was subsequently produced in medium and heavy versions (alongside some equivalent designs) to deliver more powerful explosive punch.

DID YOU KNOW?

As the war went on, an increasing percentage of personnel was devoted to manning artillery. By 1917, for example, the French had around 40 per cent of all soldiers assigned to the artillery arm, either operating the guns or performing support roles.

The most numerous category of guns on all sides was medium field artillery. These were the guns deployed within 10,000 yards (9,144m) of the fighting, to deliver direct and indirect fire support. A classic example of such a gun in British usage was the Ordnance QF ('Quick Firing') 18pdr, the standard weapon of the British Royal Field Artillery (RFA); it was also used by the Royal Horse Artillery (RHA). Manned by a six-man crew, and designed to be drawn into position behind a limber and six horses, the 18pdr was integral to the artillery fire plans during Third Ypres. The gun could fire a mix of high-explosive and shrapnel shells to a range of 5,670 yards (5,184m), and up to rates of 20rpm (although such intensive rates could not be sustained for long). To give an impression of the importance of the 18pdr to the British war effort in 1917, during that year more than 38 million shells were fired from this gun, out of 42 million manufactured.

Above the medium field guns like the 18pdr were the heavy artillery pieces, the bruising monsters capable of cracking open bunkers and delivering localised earthquakes at thousands of yards range. In the British Army, these guns were typically operated by the Royal Garrison Artillery (RGA), and the principal type was the Ordnance BL 60pdr, or 5in, gun. This thunderous gun had a range, depending on the mark of weapon and the ammunition used, of between 10,000 and 15,000 yards (9,144 and 13,716m). Rate of fire was a sedate 2rpm, but when such fire was delivered by dozens of batteries as part of an offensive battery the effects on the ground were horrendous. There were even more destructive

A Vickers machine-gun team in action; six to eight men usually operated the gun, although it could function with just two men if need be.

weapons available – such as 8in and 9.2in guns, and even 12in howitzers mounted on road or rail vehicles.

Of course, the weapons described above were just a handful of the artillery pieces roaring on the Western Front at Ypres. What made them truly effective, however, was not simply their capacity of blowing men and landscape apart, but rather their ability to be controlled in meaningful patterns and movements of fire. The directional control of artillery fire had improved immeasurably between 1914 and 1917, leading to the use of highly trained (in British terminology) Forward Observation Officers (FOOs) who could give visual adjustments to artillery from a forward position, or even from a circling aircraft.

Furthermore, artillery could be delivered in ordered and progressively moving barrages, of various types, to prepare for and support major offensives. The 'standing barrage' was the least imaginative of the barrage types – here the artillery simply hammered away at a stationary target, such as a trench line or troop concentration, hoping to neutralise it through sheer weight of shell. 'Box barrages', by contrast, bracketed a position on two or three sides, preventing enemy reinforcements from moving forward to support a position.

More advanced was the 'creeping barrage'. In this configuration, the shellfire moved forward in timed increments, for example pushed forward 50 yards (46m) every minute, with the infantry advancing closely behind. It acted as a destructive curtain that would pass over the enemy while protecting the troops following close behind. Timing and precise artillery/infantry coordination were critical. The primary goal was to allow the infantry to assault an enemy position whose occupants were still recovering from the battering they had just received. If the creeping barrage moved too far ahead of its infantry, and thus allowed the stunned occupants to come to their senses and prepare their defence, the consequences for the attackers could be appalling – the Battle of the Somme in 1916 was a case in point.

Yet eventually, the British mastered creeping barrages of baroque complexity. During the Battle of Passchendaele, for example, one artillery battery had to perform no less than forty-five distinctive 'lifts' during the bombardment. The year 1917 also saw some improvements in artillery coordination between, rather than within, divisions. Using FOOs and aircraft reconnaissance, the British artillery became better at responding in force to targets of opportunity, such as German troops massing in preparation for a counter-attack.

Artillery still had a long way to go before it reached the precision applications of the Second World War and beyond. Yet by 1917 it was certainly a multi-faceted tool of warfare. At Passchendaele, the pounding effects of artillery would be at the heart of the British tactics.

Poison Gas

By 1917, most combatant armies in the First World War had warmed to the idea of using poison gas as an offensive weapon. There were three types of gas employed: chlorine, mustard and phosgene, the delivery method being either static gas canisters (the gas was released onto the prevailing winds) or, in far smaller quantities but at a safer distance from 'friendly' troops, gas shells. Smelling something like pepper and pineapple, chlorine gas created hydrochloric acid when it came into contact with the mucosa of the lungs, causing respiratory distress and failure. Mustard gas was essentially a blistering agent, the sulphurous gas forming blisters on both exposed skin and inside the lungs. Phosgene gas was particularly insidious, attacking the system of gas exchange in the lungs and ultimately causing suffocation. The First World War was, thankfully, the first but also the last major conflict to utilise poison gas.

The result of artillery fire in Flanders.

Tactics

Several factors fed into the tactical thinking of all the armies, in 1917 on the Western Front. First and foremost were the consequences of manpower depletion, by virtue of the shocking losses of 1916, and the need to fight on multiple fronts, a situation particularly acute for the Germans. The losses of 1916 had also demanded that the combatants conserve whatever manpower was available; hence tactics became more focused on technological and manoeuvre solutions to problems, rather than just about the application of sheer manpower.

For the Germans, their tactical thinking in 1915–17 was largely defensive in nature. With so many divisions tied up on the Eastern Front, the German Army had no real option in early 1917 for a major offensive push. What it could do, however, was organise its defences to make Allied offensives costly and unproductive affairs. Thus in 1916, Germany both shortened its lines on the Western Front, to increase the concentration of defenders per mile, but also increased the depth and complexity of the defences themselves.

We should never imagine the German defensive lines as consisting of a single strong forward trench. Instead, the foremost zone (the *Vordfeldzone*) was designed to alert German forces to an attack and inflict casualties on the attackers, but was not strong enough to halt a major offensive in itself. Hence the defenders would eventually fall back into a second and stronger defensive area (the *Grosskampfzone* – battle zone) up to 3,000 yards (2,743m) further back and 1.6 miles (2.5km) deep, this area being overlooked by artillery observation positions that could call down very strong defensive fires. The second area could also mount counter-attacks at critical opportunities, just as the Allied energy was beginning to flag. Even further back was a *rückwärtige Kampfzone* (rear battle zone), holding a battalion of each regiment in reserve, ready to surge forward when required.

Note how here we use the word 'area' rather than line. Indeed, the deep, multi-layer German defensive zone was a decentralised and staggered space (divisional and battalion commands were now more important to battlefield decisions than corps and army commands), with multiple *Widerstandsnester* ('resistance nests' or strongpoints) dotting the landscape to form breakwaters for the Allied attackers.

By forcing the Allies to attack through miles of defences, and with plenty of troops held back for the opportune counter-attack, the Germans had put in place the perfect counter to Allied infantry assaults, plus they maximised the chances of their troops surviving the artillery fire on which the Allied had increasingly come to rely. The details of what is known as the 'elastic defence' or 'defence in depth' were adjusted constantly to meet the demands of the campaign.

The British, by contrast, were still wedded to offensive thinking, and as the French fell into a stunned recovery phase after the traumas of 1916, the BEF was increasingly called upon to shoulder the burdens of combat on the Western Front. To support attacks, artillery control had developed ever greater levels of sophistication. Now, artillery fires could be coordinated both between and within corps, providing for a more concerted programme of fire across an entire battlefront. Furthermore, divisional commanders could also call on extra batteries to bring down specific fire when needed, meaning that the artillery could respond flexibly to developing threats during the course of an attack.

For the infantry, everything had changed tactically. Gone were the days of walking methodically across the battlefield in serried ranks; now manoeuvre and tempo were the keywords. Platoons were divided into four specialist sections: 1) grenade throwers; 2) Lewis gun (one gunner and several assistants); 3) sniper, scout and riflemen; and 4) soldiers armed with rifle grenades. Together these four sections could act in fast-moving and mutually supportive roles on the battlefield, with the Lewis gunner and rifle grenades providing covering fire when resistance was met, while the two other sections surged forward to clear trench lines and positions.

Furthermore, while some platoons might find themselves engaged in taking or consolidating positions, other platoons could push straight through if opportunity presented itself, surging forward to maintain the operation tempo. Although investment was made in increasing the flow of communication from the front of the offensive back to the headquarters, platoons and companies now enjoyed more independent tactical thinking, as long as they were operating within the overall confines of the general plan.

A Lewis gunner trains his machine gun skyward as an anti-aircraft weapon, aiming to bring down German reconnaissance and fighter planes.

So what we have at Third Ypres are two very different systems coming into contact. On the one side, we have the Germans operating defence-in-depth principles, designed to sap the momentum from an enemy attack and then surge back forward to reclaim any ground lost. On the other, the British were focusing on a greater flexibility in tactical manoeuvre.

We must not, however, think that the British were operating in a vacuum in their development of infantry tactics. In fact, both the French and the Germans had also been developing more effective and flexible assault tactics as far back as 1915. The French had, in many ways, pioneered coordination between rifle-grenades and LMGs, and the Germans' ability to respond with vigorous counter-attacks relied upon fast-moving independent units ready to seize ground where they saw enemy weaknesses.

Passchendaele would be a meeting ground for these various tactical perspectives. As we shall see, however, there is a world of difference between a tactical plan drawn out neatly on paper, and that which has to be executed on a real-world landscape against opponents fighting for their lives.

THE DAYS
BEFORE BATTLE

For the British soldier, life at Ypres between major offensives reflected that of soldiers elsewhere on the Western Front. The Tommy did not spend all his deployment in the front-line trenches – far from it. In fact, he was regularly rotated out of the front line to safer areas in the rear.

For those behind the lines, time was passed either in mundane garrison, training or drill duties, or, if the soldier was on leave, enjoying himself in whatever Belgian or French town provided rest and recreation. At Ypres, a major destination and transit point was Poperinghe, 7 miles (11km) to the west of Ypres. Poperinghe not only billeted large numbers of troops (at least a division at any one time), it was also a social centre for the soldiers from the front-line positions, and from any of the dozens of camps in the town's vicinity.

Clubs and bars for officers and men proliferated, some becoming famous institutions throughout the British Army. The most popular venue was Talbot House ('Toc H'), a true everyman's club. Thousands of British soldiers drank and slept in Talbot House, and such was the quality of its restitution that General Plumer later commented: 'In all my experience I have never known a place so vital to morale as Talbot House.' Of course, there were plenty of alternative lures in Poperinghe; the proliferation of bars,

DID YOU KNOW?

Some calculations suggest that only 15 per cent of the entire time a British soldier spent on the Western Front was endured in the firing-line trenches. Forty per cent was actually sat out in either support trenches or (even further back) reserve trenches, while 45 per cent was mercifully out of the trenches, enjoying life in the rear areas.

hotels, restaurants, brothels and other attractions leading some soldiers to believe that they had arrived in Paris when transiting to and from the front. Yet in the early summer of 1917, it would have been readily apparent that those enjoying themselves in Poperinghe were doing so with an air of nervousness at what was to come.

Planning the Battle

On 7 June 1917, nineteen vast underground explosions lifted thousands of tons of Belgian earth into the sky in Flanders. The explosives had been planted in tunnels, dug by specialist British Army tunnellers, which ran up to 100ft (32m) below the German front-line trenches on Messines Ridge, to the south of the Ypres Salient. The detonations were truly dreadful – they were so loud that they were heard in southern Britain, and in those horrible instants some 10,000 German soldiers were killed, torn apart by the blast or buried alive by the displacement of earth.

The explosions were the inaugural act to the Messines Offensive, a British attack designed to take the Messines Ridge from German hands and thus straighten out the Ypres Salient, while also making the salient itself a more secure launch pad for future offensives in Flanders. The offensive was a stunning success. Those Germans not killed or wounded by the mine explosions, or by the 2,250-gun preparatory barrage that followed immediately in their wake, put up weak resistance in the face of an attack by X (British) Corps and II ANZAC Corps, and by mid-afternoon the whole of the ridge was in British hands, with Messines and Wytschaete coming back into Allied possession.

The pressure was maintained, and on 11 June the Germans were in general withdrawal throughout the sector. Thus by mid-June, the Ypres line was dramatically straightened, running in a roughly straight line from around Hooge in the north, to Armentières in the south.

Here was a dramatic moment of opportunity for Haig. With the Germans in disarray, this would have been the perfect moment to launch the general Flanders offensive. Yet in reality, there would be another eight weeks before the offensive at Ypres – the delays caused by logistical issues amongst the French First Army and Gough's Fifth Army. During this time, the German Fourth Army consolidated its defences in front of Ypres, in full expectation of a further offensive.

There were some turbulent arguments amongst the German high command, revolving around the exact nature of the defensive arrangements, but operational orders were eventually issued on 27 June. The backstop of the German positions was *Flandern I*, one of three intended defensive lines in Flanders, the construction of which began in February 1917. (*Flandern I* was the only line actually completed by the beginning of the Ypres offensive.)

A British howitzer opens up at the battle of Messines Ridge, the highly successful precursor action to the Battle of Third Ypres. During the battle, the British managed to straighten out the southern edge of the Ypres Salient.

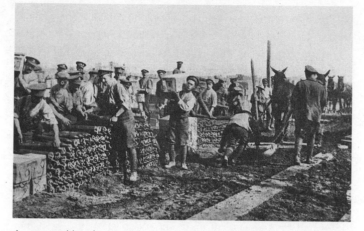

An ammunition dump on the Menin Road, with the ground being prepared for more supplies. The combined British artillery offensive at Third Ypres expended hundreds of thousands of shells monthly.

The line ran along the Passchendaele Ridge and through Broodseinde. In front of it were three lines/zones of German defences. The foremost of the lines was a string of rather lightly defended breastworks, but 2,000 yards (1,829m) behind these was the far more heavily defended Albrecht Line, featuring strongpoints plus German assault troops ready to surge forward into the counter-attack, supported by a network of HMGs with interlocking fields of fire. The German main battle zone, of which the Albrecht Line was the frontal component, was about 2,000 yards (1,892m) deep, behind which were the pillboxes and reserve battalions manning the Wilhelm Line. Between the Wilhelm Line and *Flandern I* were assembly areas for *Eingreif* divisions, which also had the purpose of counter-attacking to block and turn enemy breakthroughs.

The German preparations for an Ypres offensive were formidable, and were made possible by the tardiness of the planning and preparation for Passchendaele attack. On 14 June, nevertheless, Haig had outlined his immediate plans for the Ypres offensive in more detail:

Underlying the general intention of wearing out the enemy is the strategical idea of securing the Belgian coast and connecting our front with the Dutch frontier. The nature and size of the several steps which we take towards that objective must depend upon our *effectives* and the replacement of *guns*. Roughly these steps are:

A   Capture the bridgehead formed by the Passchendaele–Staden–Clercken ridge.
B   Push on towards Roulers–Thourout, so as to take the German coast defences in the rear.
C   Land by surprise on the Ostend front in conjunction with an attack from Nieuport.

If our effectives or guns are inadequate, and progress is delayed, it may be necessary to call a half after A is gained.

Douglas Haig, 14 June 1917.

The finer details of this plan were thrashed out during the remainder of June and into July, and were outlined in a paper from Haig to his army commanders on 5 July. Because this forms a useful framework for much of the subsequent discussion of the campaign, it is worth quoting in detail:

2   The Fifth Army, assisted on its right by the Second Army and co-operating on its left with the French and the Belgians, is first to secure the PASSCHENDAELE–STADEN RIDGE. To drive the enemy off that Ridge from STIRLING CASTLE in the south to DIXMUDE in the north is likely to entail very hard fighting lasting perhaps for weeks; but as a result of this we may hope that our subsequent progress will be more rapid.

3   Subject to the modifications necessitated by developments in the situation, the next effort of the Fifth Army, with the French and the Belgians, – after gaining the Ridge – mentioned above – will be directed north-eastwards to gain the line (approximately) THOUROUT–COUELAERE.

4   Simultaneously with this advance to the THOUROUT–COUELAERE line the Fourth Army, acting in combination with naval forces, will attack the enemy about NIEUPORT and on the cast to the east of there.

5   The Fourth Army and the forces attacking the line THOUROUT–COUELAERE will afterwards operate to join hands on the general line THOUROUT–OSTEND and to push on to BRUGES.

6   Operations eastwards, and towards LICHTERVELDE, from the PASSCHENDAELE–STADEN Ridge will be required to cover the right flank of the advance on THOUROUT; and possession of the high ground between THOUROUT and ROULERS will be of importance subsequently to cover the flank of the advance on BRUGES.

7   In the operations subsequent to the capture of the PASSCHENDAELE–STADEN Ridge opportunities for the employment of Cavalry in masses are likely to offer.

8   The Second Army will cover and co-operate with the right flank of the Fifth Army as already ordered and will be prepared to take over gradually the defence of the main Ridge from the Fifth Army, possibly as far as PASSCHENDAELE or even to a further point. The Commander of the Second Army will also be prepared with plans to develop an advance towards the line WARNETON–MENIN, or to push forward on the right of the Fifth Army to the line COURTRAI–ROULERS (throwing out a flank guard along the line of the LYS), if circumstances should render such movements desirable as the situation develops.

9   As far as can be foreseen at present the main operation after the capture of the STIRLING CASTLE–PASSCHENDAELE–DIXMUDE Ridge will be those directed toward OSTEND and BRUGES.

Douglas Haig, 5 July 1917.

This long passage fully conveys Haig's bold ambitions for the Flanders offensive, which not only breaks out of the Ypres Salient but also ultimately (although 'as far as can be foreseen') include the capture of Ostend and Bruges, effectively breaking the German hold over Belgium. It was hoped, the Ypres offensive would tip the tide of was on the Western Front.

Preparations

By early July the preparations for the forthcoming offensive were well under way. Thousands of tons of ammunition were pushed up to the artillery batteries, to fuel them not only for the preparatory bombardment but also for the sustained artillery fire that would be required to keep the offensive supported. The supply journeys themselves were hazardous enterprises, as is explained by the testimony of driver L.G. Burton, 40th Division, Motor Transport:

> If the attack was going to work at all we had to get big loads of supplies right up to the front line before the offensive. I was with a motor lorry ammunition column and our job was to get the stuff up. We took up everything – shells, rifle ammunition, Mills hand-grenades, mortar bombs, duckboards, narrow-gauge railway-line sections, wood and loads of large gas or liquid-fire cylinders. Day and night we worked from dumps to depots and depots to dumps near the front fighting line. We used to go through Ypres at night with no lights on our lorries, of course, as the road was under enemy observation from the various hills around. But there would be plenty of Very lights from the fronts going up and down continuously all around us, the flashes from our own guns and Howitzers in the ruins, and enemy shells bursting among the wrecked houses and roads. It was just fumes and dust and smells all the time, and sometimes there was gas too, sometimes incendiary shells. You could see them glowing red among the brick-ends.
>
> L.G. Burton, quoted in MacDonald, *Passchendaele*, p.95.

British soldiers, on a canal in Flanders, bring up supplies to the front line. The canal network provided a useful north–south supply route through Ypres.

The supply runs to the front were all conducted under the eyes and shells of the German artillery, the British artillery responding in kind. For even in the pre-offensive days, the British guns were kept heavily engaged with counter-battery duties. The Germans, in full expectation of an offensive at Ypres, had stepped up their own artillery fire, disrupting the British preparations as well as inflicting not insubstantial casualties on the Allied troops. Captain J.L. Jack, an officer in the 1st Cameronians, made this note in his diary, dated 22 July 1917:

> The German shell fire on Ypres is persistent and heavy in reply to terrific poundings by our own artillery. Shell splinters and masonry are constantly flying about while the concussion

seldom ceases altogether. All troops not on duty must remain under cover; but even so, the casualties in and around the town are severe, amounting, I believe, to 400 or 500 daily. Between dusk and dawn working and carrying parties, as well as transport bringing stores along the Poperinghe road into Ypres, have nerve-wracking experiences in this ghastly area …

Our office is in a tin hut a few yards from the ramparts into which we may adjourn when the fire becomes too hot. Concealed amid the ruins near us are some 8-inch howitzers, two of which lie overturned in their shattered emplacements.

J.L. Jack, 22 July 1917.

Further diary entries on both sides reveal the terrifying intensity of the artillery duel in the second half of July. The British shelling of German lines was described as a steady crescendo, reaching more than 10 miles (16km) into the German rear-areas in an attempt to disrupt and smash the integrity of German defensive responses. The Germans themselves were all too aware that they were being prepared for a forthcoming offensive. German general, Hermann von Kuhl, who served at Third Ypres, later noted in *Der Weltkrieg, 1914 bis 1918*: 'The signs that intensive and long lasting battles were ahead were clearly visible. The main effort would be in the Flanders.'

'Clearly visible' they were, and any attempt by the British to hide the fact was futile, although the diary of one Belgian civilian, Pastor von Walleghem, shows that there was still a pretence at military secrecy:

9 July 1917. There is more and more talk about the impending offensive, we see many extensive preparations here, and learn the ones of the neighbouring sectors; additional railways are being laid all around. Guns are being brought in and the ammunition depots are being enlarged and new ones established. Soldiers and officers alike tell the civilians that it will be terrible and continuous. They must break through at any

cost, and in a few short weeks Flanders will be delivered. Also the newspapers make mention of the importance of the coming offensive. The people are full of hope, but those nearest the front fear the bombing which will precede the battle. Under the circumstances, a farmer from Vlamertinghe requests permission from the military authorities to move his livestock owing to the danger of the coming offensive. Instead of obtaining this he received a visit from the Gendarmes: 'What? An impending offensive? How do you know that? How dare you give away military preparations!'

Pastor von Walleghem, quoted in MacDonald,
Passchendaele, p.87.

With the Flanders offensive being such common knowledge, it is clear that the only elements that Haig could hope to conceal from the Germans was the exact time and day of the offensive, plus the basic delineations of attack routes. Yet given the nature of the Ypres Salient, the German planners could be reasonably confident of where the British thrust would fall most heavily. Now both sides waited for the inevitable, monstrous clash.

Stacks of artillery shells wait to be dispatched to battle. A shortage of artillery shells in 1915 precipitated the 'shell crisis', a political storm that contributed to the fall of the Asquith government in 1916.

THE BATTLEFIELD:
WHAT ACTUALLY HAPPENED?

On the evening of 30 July 1917, all British forces were in their place around the Ypres Salient, hearts thumping hard and anxiously behind khaki tunics. On paper, things looked good for Haig, at least in terms of numerical superiority. In the far north of the attack front, above Ypres, were six Belgian divisions and also six French divisions of the French First Army, under Anthoine. They faced the German Group Dixmude, which was two divisions strong. Around Ypres itself, and forming the main component of the offensive, was Gough's Fifth Army. In total, Gough had eighteen divisions at his disposal, as compared to the five divisions of Group Ypres opposite. Forming the British right was Plumer's Second Army, twelve divisions against the six divisions of Group Wytschaete. With such a preponderance of divisions, some degree of Allied confidence was warranted, although the Germans had become the undoubted masters of the trenchant defence.

Via discussions between Haig, Gough and Plumer, the British objectives for the first day of the offensive were set. In their broadest terms, the Fifth Army was tasked with moving forward and securing the uplands situated to the east and north-east of Ypres (the Passchendaele–Staden Ridge).

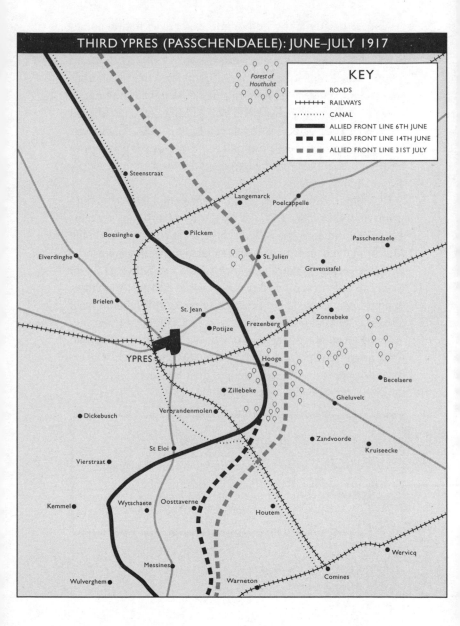

THIRD YPRES (PASSCHENDAELE): JUNE–JULY 1917

KEY

ROADS
++++++ RAILWAYS
·········· CANAL
▬▬▬ ALLIED FRONT LINE 6TH JUNE
▬ ▬ ▬ ALLIED FRONT LINE 14TH JUNE
▬ ▬ ▬ ALLIED FRONT LINE 31ST JULY

Forest of Houthulst

Steenstraat

Langemarck

Poelcappelle

Boesinghe

Pilckem

Passchendaele

Elverdinghe

St. Julien

Gravenstafel

Brielen

St. Jean

Potijze

Frezenberg

Zonnebeke

YPRES

Hooge

Becelaere

Zillebeke

Gheluvelt

Dickebusch

Verbrandenmolen

Zandvoorde

Kruiseecke

St Eloi

Vierstraat

Kemmel

Wytschaete

Oosttaverne

Houtem

Wervicq

Messines

Warneton

Comines

Wulverghem

Across the front, the immediate objectives had been set in terms of three main lines of advance forward. The blue, black and green lines were progressively 1,000, 2,000 and 3,500 yards (914m, 1,828m and 3,200m) from the British front line, and if the green line were reached then the advance would have pushed through the German Wilhelm Line. An optimistic red line was also delineated on the maps, a further 1,000–1,500 yards (914–1,372m) deeper into German territory, but this was only to be attempted if the opportunity presented itself to some plucky divisional commander.

The infantry assault itself would be preceded by a six-minute storm of artillery fire, delivered by a total of 1,164 heavy guns and 1,592 field guns (the bulk of which were concentrated in the Fifth Army), the infantry would then launch the attack behind a protective creeping barrage, which would lift 100 yards (91m) every four minutes to make progress. Note also that the British offensive would have the support of some 120 Mk IV tanks, with forty-eight held in reserve.

Three Allied armies faced a single, albeit prepared, German Army across the Ypres battle lines. At 0350 hrs on 31 July 1917, the battle commenced – few people then foresaw that it would still be rumbling on four months later.

DID YOU KNOW?

The Mk IV tank had a crew of no fewer than eight men, and was armed with two 6pdr guns in its 'male' version. Top speed was a less than impressive 4mph (6.4km/h).

The Battle of Pilckem Ridge

At 0350 hrs, as planned, the British artillery unleashed a hellish barrage on the German defenders opposite. From the surviving accounts, it seems that this bombardment was almost as unnerving to many of the attackers as it was to the enemy, as the following diary entry from a British soldier testifies:

> Never-ending howls and piercing screams are rending the air from the sea to the River Lys, while accessory noises like growls and blows seem to spring from everywhere on the Yser, in front of Dixmude and Langemarck, around Hollebeke and Warneton. The whole of West Flanders is one large, steaming pot, in which death and devastation are brewing. With the sun smiling its brightest at us, terrific, never-ending thunderstorms are raging over the land. Amid noises such as the old earth never heard before, a crop of new battles and new wars between nations is growing to maturity.
>
> Horne, *Source Records*.

The pounding lasted for a few minutes, then the whistles blew and the infantry surged over the top of their trenches. The Battle of Third Ypres was now underway.

This opening action in the campaign came to be known as the Battle of Pilckem Ridge. In the far north of the British sector was the Guards Division, who pushed forward in the face of, initially, light resistance. The three Guards divisions reached their blue line objectives in a matter of minutes, and their black line objectives in a few hours, although resistance strengthened from German machine guns emplaced in blockhouses along the Ypres–Staden Railway and in Abri Wood.

The 2nd Guards Brigade managed to take out the blockhouses along the railway, while the 4th Grenadier Guards dealt with the threat from Abri Wood. The advances in this sector went on. In fact, by the early afternoon most of the XIV Corps objectives (the

Wounded soldiers lie in a dressing station awaiting treatment after the Battle of Pilckem Ridge, 31 July–2 August 1917.

Wounded British soldiers at Pilckem Ridge. Chances of surviving serious wounds improved if the soldiers made it back to a Casualty Clearing Station, a more advanced aid post behind the front line.

Guards and 38th Divisions) up to the green line had been taken. The 38th Division, for example, had pushed through Pilckem and onto the ridge beyond, with the 115th Brigade advancing through to the Steenbeek. This constituted an advance of 2.5 miles (4km).

Probably the most concerning issue encountered by XIV Corps, and one that was beginning to affect the whole front, was the weather. The Ypres sector would receive a hefty 0.8in (21.7mm) of rain on 31 July (more than had fallen in all the preceding days of the month), making the battlefield muddy and treacherous. There would be rain on all but two of the first ten days of August over Passchendaele, and the contribution of weather to the progress of the campaign would become dominant over subsequent weeks and months.

The environmental conditions were felt especially by the British tanks, which were attempting to grind their way across sodden, tractionless landscapes that had most of their navigable landmarks stripped from them by the preparatory shellfire. In the XVIII Corps sector, many of the tanks were left as immobile iron hulls stuck in the mud, having been unable to make a meaningful contribution to the battle. Their situation, and that of the infantry accompanying them, was made more problematic by the Steenbeek stream that ran between the German second and third lines. Once shells had broken the banks of the stream open, the battlefield became a soaking morass. Added to this was the fact that, by around 0500 hrs, the German artillery was beginning to recover and get into its stride, dropping a heavy weight of shells onto the British advance.

Despite such obstacles, XVIII Corps managed to make a successful advance, establishing itself on the Steenbeek from St Julien (captured by the 116th Brigade) to the Pilckem–Langemark road, with the 4/5th Black Watch pushing across the stream to assault the ridge beyond. Using a judicious combination of tank power, artillery and infantry manoeuvre, 117th Brigade captured three pillboxes at Regina Cross and a strongpoint at Alberta. Although XVIII Corps managed to put down roots across the stream, they also faced more vigorous German counter-attacks later in the day, and took heavy casualties from German machine guns around Kitchener's Wood. The 118th Brigade also had to withdraw from St Julien to the Steenbeek after the slower advance of the 55th Division on their right exposed the brigade's flank.

In the XIX Corps sector, progress on that first day of battle was punishing but promising. The primary objective of the 15th Division was the Frezenburg Ridge (the black line) then through the Steenbeek Valley to the green line. Frezenburg village was taken, and a German counter-attack at 0830 hrs was beaten back by the 44th and 46th Brigades. The 55th Division pushed out from Wieltje, with some elements advancing as far as the green line. However, fortified farms, such as Plum Farm, Square Farm, Spree Farm and Pond Farm, were causing the Allies some heavy bruising. Although the British managed to take several of these strongpoints, by the end of the day many remained in German hands, proving the efficiency of the German model of defence in depth.

The 8th Division around Hooge had a tough day. The strength of the German resistance in this sector, particularly in terms of enfilading machine-gun fire from Nonne Bosschen and Glencorse Wood, meant that the energy drained out of the attack. German counter-attacks in the sector were also effective, so although the division had reached the blue and black lines with relative ease, the 23rd and 24th Brigades were eventually forced back to take shelter on the Westhoek Ridge.

Of all the corps committed to battle on 31 July however, it was probably II Corps that had the most arduous push forward, across the well-defended Gheluvelt Plateau. The German defences were at their strongest around this stretch of the line, and the enemy also had substantial *Eingreif* reserves that they could commit when necessary.

The three brigades (17th, 72nd and 73rd) of the 24th Division attacked outwards from positions around Klein Zillebeke and into Shrewsbury Forest, facing fierce resistance at locations such as Lower Star Post, Tower Hamlets and Jordan Trench. Although the brigades managed to take most of their blue line objectives, the black line was more problematic, and the brigades had to consolidate short of their goals (the 72nd Brigade even had to pull back to positions short of the blue line, in the face of German counter-attacks).

The 30th Division, meanwhile, took more than two hours to struggle through the shattered remnants of Sanctuary Wood. The 21st Brigade managed to capture Stirling Castle Ridge (although only with reinforcements from 89th Brigade). In the confusion of terrain and battle, some 90th Brigade troops attacked and captured Chateau Wood in the belief that it was Glencorse Wood. Therefore, the 53rd Brigade, 18th Division, went towards Glencorse Wood expecting it to be in friendly hands, but instead found heavy resistance, and by 1000 hrs had been forced to dig in in positions north-west of the wood.

German artillery fire also increased in both its intensity and accuracy during the day, inflicting a horrible toll on the soldiers struggling to make their way over a muddy landscape.

It was not only the British who were pushing ahead against resistance from both climate and the Germans. In the north, the French were attacking along a 3,000-yard (2,743m) front, pushing off across the Yser Canal, using a total of thirty-nine bridges laid in advance. As with the British experience, the French initially made good progress, going on to take Bixschoote and Kortekeer Kabaret, but then the drenched landscape and strong German counter-attacks in the afternoon took the momentum out of the push. The French, therefore, dug in, an effort that was physically traumatic given that the ground was essentially a crumbling, sodden mass.

An Infantryman's Diary, 31 July 1917

This battle has lasted for days; now it is again that continuous roar that effaces, or rather, consumes, all individual noises, that makes even fierce explosions close by you indistinguishable. Everything disappears in one loud, rolling, threatening volume of sound. The air carries it a hundred miles distant, and tremblingly they listen, south and north, west and east, where they cannot see the horror of all this.

But if you come nearer, it is like the bowels of the earth exploding. Our soldiers sit in their dugouts, and cannot do anything but trust to luck. Just now the infantry must keep quiet; only the big guns are talking. The waiting infantry is, as it were, locked in prison. The men cannot get out, nor can anybody approach them. The way to them is fraught with fearful danger.

All around spatter steel splinters, shrapnel bullets, stones and earth. If you are hit you are dead or crippled. What shall one do? One smokes incessantly, until the air in the narrow shaft is heavy enough to cut. That is bad, but somehow it helps one to endure the horrors of the situation.

Horne, *Source Records.*

The Battlefield: What Actually Happened?

At the opposite end of the battlefield was the British Second Army, with its major ANZAC contingent. In essence, the Second Army's attacks were meant to act as a draw on German forces further north, through an Allied attack on the Warneton–Zandvoorde line. IX Corps made decent advances on the first day of battle, captured objectives including La Basse Ville (by the New Zealand Division) and Junction Buildings, Tiny Farm and Spider Farm by the 56th Brigade. German resistance, in the form of rolling counter-attacks, stiffened around 0730 hrs, and there began a bloody pushing and pulling for scraps of ground in the IX Corps sector. Some battalions were pushed back, but the corps as a whole was able to consolidate its ground as day turned into night.

X Corps was tested sorely in its attack against the German positions. The 41st Division, for example, had an axis of attack along the Yser–Comines Canal. During this advance, it faced devastating machine-gun fire from both left and right flanks, plus lethal German artillery fire. (The 41st had already lost hundreds of men to German artillery during the forming up period in the days leading up to the attack.) By the end of the day, the division as a whole had managed to advance just 650 yards (594m), although some battalions had got to within 100 yards (91m) of the green line.

The tactical picture of the first forty-eight hours of Third Ypres is a complicated one, with dozens of minor actions rippling up and down the front, the Germans attempting to reclaim lost territory, and the British pushed back and forward. Gough, aware of the staggered progress behind made by the British formations, ordered XIX Corps to push on to the green line, but this plan was stopped by German counter-attacks, which became more general and more powerful from around 1400 hrs. The British forces were gradually pushed back from the green line acquisitions, paid for in blood just hours earlier. The retreat in the centre of the Allied offensives eventually stopped just short of the black line; it was progress in the XVII and XIX Corps sectors that most concerned the Germans, hence they received heavy counter-assaults. St Julien fell once again into German hands as the line contracted.

The attack/counter-attack pattern was repeated over the coming week, although from 2 August the adjustments were minor. The green line objectives now lay in the distance for the Allies, and the Germans remained in possession of much of the key high ground. Yet Haig felt that there was plenty to celebrate. Despite the fact that the Allies had lost nearly 32,000 casualties between 31 July and 2 August, they had secured the German first-line defences. The Germans had also taken about 30,000 casualties, but most of theirs had been incurred during the preparatory bombardment phase from 21 to 31 July. Although the Allies had made advances at times that were greater than allowed by the Fourth Army's defensive strategy, von Arnim's counter-strokes had gone a long way to restoring the situation.

In addition, both sides were now contesting with an unforgiving enemy – the weather. The extremely heavy summer rains, combined with the ground-churning effects of the heavy shellfire, had turned the landscape into a tortured and soaking quagmire. This presented major problems in terms of consolidating ground. Trenches collapsed constantly, or filled up rapidly with water if good drainage could not be achieved. William Beach Thomas, writing for the *Daily Mail*, reflected soberly on the conditions:

Floods of rain and a blanket of mist have doused and cloaked the whole of the Flanders plain. The rain has so fouled this low, stoneless ground, spoiled of all natural drainage by shell-fire, that we experienced the double value of the early work, for today moving heavy material was extremely difficult and the men could scarcely walk in full equipment, much less dig. Every man was soaked through and was standing or sleeping in a marsh. It was a work of energy to keep a rifle in a state fit to use.

Daily Mail, 2 August 1917.

The exhaustion that Thomas focuses on would become a major factor in the development of the Battle of Third Ypres. The mud imposed a massive inertia, an extra level of effort applied to every operation or task, which in turn slowed the possible tempo of operations. Another journalist, the American Percival Phillips, also saw the depredations of the weather, although noted that it affected all sides in the battle:

> The weather changed for the worse last night, although fortunately too late to hamper the execution of our plans. The rain was heavy and constant throughout the night. It was still beating down steadily when the day broke chill and cheerless, with a thick blanket of mist completely shutting off the battlefield. During the morning it slackened to a dismal drizzle, but by this time the roads, fields, and footways were covered with semi-liquid mud, and the torn ground beyond Ypres had become in places a horrible quagmire.
>
> It was pretty bad in the opinion of the weary soldiers who came back with wounds, but it was certainly worse for the enemy holding fragments of broken lines still heavily hammered by the artillery and undoubtedly disheartened by the hardships of a wet night in the open after a day of defeat.
>
> *Daily Express*, 2 August 1917.

The weather would not always be so inclement. During August there would be some bone-dry and hot days that would afflict men with dust and thirst more than sodden clothes and chills. Yet the weather would become almost a combatant in itself over the subsequent months.

Timeline

Westhoek and Langemarck

From 3–10 August, the appalling weather in Flanders limited the tactical options of both sides, although fighting rumbled in on various sectors throughout most days. However, a gradually drying battlefield meant that on 10 August the British were able to resume some of their offensive initiative, with an effort to take strong German positions on the well-defended Gheluvelt Plateau. In the early hours of the morning, the 18th and 24th Divisions

DID YOU KNOW?

Siegfried Sassoon's poem 'Memorial Tablet' (1918)
includes the lines:

Squire nagged and bullied till I went to fight,
(Under Lord Derby's scheme). I died in hell –
(They called it Passchèndaele). My wound was slight,
And I was hobbling back; and then a shell
Burst slick upon the duckboards: so I fell
Into the bottomless mud, and lost the light.

committed themselves to battle once again, this time aiming to claim Westhoek Ridge and village, plus clear the Germans from positions in Inverness Copse and Glencorse Wood, two obstinate objectives in the centre of the Ypres operation.

The attacks had mixed results. The 18th's attempt to secure Inverness Copse and Glencorse Wood began promisingly, but largely ended in failure when a powerful German counter-attack drove the division from its gains, leaving only a small north-west corner of Glencorse Wood in British hands.

Better results were had from the attack up Westhoek Ridge. The remainder of the ridge plus the village were claimed, ejecting the German garrison there, but at the cost of nearly 1,500 casualties, including 158 dead and 100 missing. The German forces, infuriated at the loss of Westhoek, kept pressure on the beleaguered 25th Division through the night and into the following days, but the soldiers held on and were relieved by the 8th and 56th Divisions on 14 August.

The battle around Ypres was only a week old when political grumblings began about its lack of progress. Although Haig had been largely upbeat about its progress, the fact remained that most of its initial objectives lay out of reach and across ground now littered with Allied bodies. The counter-attack responses of the German Fourth Army proved to be consistently effective, and

Ammunition is transported forward by rail during the Battle of Langemarck. The British creeping barrage was reduced in effect by the terrible weather conditions.

the weather had imposed conditions that made long-distance advances highly unlikely.

Most worrying for Haig was a comment made by Lloyd George on 7 August at a conference in London. Speaking with international delegates about where to channel British reinforcements, he said of the Flanders operation: 'I am afraid that we have put our money on the wrong horse. It would have been better to have reinforced the Italians.' This frank critique was relayed to Haig, who was incensed. What Haig felt the Ypres operation required was not critical remarks, but continued and committed logistical support to keep up the pressure on the Germans.

That pressure would come in the form of a new offensive, scheduled to start on 16 August. In essence, the plan was for II, XVIII and XIX Corps to push on to the green line objectives that had so far eluded them, and in the process take the strategic position of Langemarck. The mission of II Corps was to move forward by about 1,600 yards (1,463m), focusing on taking Polygon Wood, while the 8th Division punched beyond the green line on a front between Westhoek and the Ypres–Roulers railway.

Further north, the drive to the green line by XVIII and XIX Corps would include the capture of the Langemarck itself by the 20th Division, using its 60th and 61st Brigades. The plan was for the 60th Brigade to move around Langemarck on the right, forming a protective barrier against the near-certain possibility that the Germans would launch a counter-attack from positions about 1.5 miles (2.4km) up the road at Poelcappelle. The 61st Brigade, meanwhile, could go at the village head on, capturing it from the German garrison while under the shield of the 60th Brigade.

Overall, the Allied forces concentrated for the Langemarck offensive were given three lines of objectives – blue, green and red – blue being the most proximate and red being the most distant. As with the previous British operations, the British troops would also have the benefit of well-coordinated artillery support at every stage. Creeping barrages would protect the infantry during advances, while standing barrages would deliver extreme fire effects upon the German lines, softening them up for the

British and French artillery observers at the Battle of Langemarck. Their role was to observe the fall of the shot and provide range and traverse adjustments and timing instructions to bring it onto target.

British infantry. Smoke barrages would also be used to provide a screen behind which the soldiers could consolidate positions once captured, and form up to prepare for the next assault.

As ever, the Germans were perfectly aware of the likely routes of future British attacks, and had prepared themselves accordingly in the Langemarck area. Yet the state of the German troops was a cause for concern for the German high command. Two weeks of constant fighting had depleted many divisions severely, typically to the tune of 1,500–2,000 men lost. Furthermore, like the Allies, the Germans were becoming exhausted having to wrestle with the effects of mud.

Judging to what extent the German morale was collapsing is hard to assess. Some Fifth Army reports noted that 'the general morale of the Germans is undoubtedly lowered' while a note in the diary of one Colonel Macleod on 15 August explained that 'The Bosches are fighting with the utmost stubbornness. Their morale does not appear to be bad and their troops seem well fed, so they are nowhere near cracking yet.' Probably the variation in such reports stems from the danger of making general deductions from local evidence. Doubtless the morale of the German troops varied from unit to unit, depending on factors such as the exhaustion of the men involved and the quality of their leadership.

The Battle of Langemarck, as this phase of Third Ypres is known, began at 0445 hrs with the customary, but ever-brutal, artillery bombardment. However, it should be noted that during the previous days British engineers had to perform near miracles in creating bridges across the Steenbeek, to enable the British troops to make a convincing jump off. Some hard local actions had been fought on the east bank of the Steenbeek on the 15th, to consolidate the ground for the offensive. One officer, Captain A. Goring of C Company, 6th Battalion, the Yorkshire Regiment, was a member of a wire-cutting party, which ended up in perilous position under fire from German small arms. His attempt to raise some artillery support demonstrates just one of the many peculiar effects that the weather was having on operations:

I wanted to send a message back to see if we could get a bit of help from the artillery. We had two pigeons in a basket, but the trouble was that the wretched birds had got soaked when the platoon floundered into the flooded ground. We tried to dry one of them off as best we could and I wrote a message, attached it to its leg and sent it off. To our absolute horror the bird was so wet that it just flapped into the air and then came straight down again, and started actually walking towards the German line about a hundred yards away. Well, if the message had got into the Germans' hands, they would have known that we were on our own and we'd have been in real trouble. So we had to try to shoot the pigeon before it got there.

A. Goring.

The episode with the unfortunate pigeon must have been repeated hundreds of times during the Battle of Third Ypres, added to which there were the problems of installing and maintaining electrical communications through a soaked battlefield. On several occasions we see reports acknowledging that, in the absence of clear communications, it was actually hard to tell what was going on at the front. Such poor communications can only have added to the casualties of this prolonged campaign.

At 0445 hrs, the British barrage was delivered, and the new phase of the British offensive began. Having crossed the Steenbeek, the soldiers of II Corps stepped forward into the German defence. If German morale was low, it didn't appear to have affected their ability to put down terrifyingly heavy machine-gun fire. The 53rd Brigade made agonisingly slow progress under hails of 7.92mm rounds, the terrain meaning that the brigade had no support from the planned tank elements. Nevertheless, various lines of advance by II Corps forces coalesced on Glencorse Wood, leading to the Germans finally being ejected from this area. The British troops then pushed on forwards to Polygon Wood, although increasingly the mud was physically dictating the tactical movement of entire formations, resulting in some worrying gaps opening up in the lines of advance. Furthermore, because of the mud the British were deprived of tank support during the battle, making the job of crushing strongpoints that much more difficult.

Meanwhile, the 8th Division was also, initially, forging ahead. It also had a water obstacle to negotiate – the Hanebeek – across which engineers had laid bridges for the infantry to cross. Strongpoints captured included Iron Cross, Anzac Redoubt and Zonnebeke Redoubt, but as the day wore on the 8th made greater progress than the 16th and 56th Divisions on either flank, leaving it exposed to flanking fire from German machine guns and field artillery.

The XIX Corps (which included the 16th and 36th Divisions), also focused its efforts on the Anzac and Zonnebeke Redoubts but, within a few hundred yards of setting out, ran into serious trouble from machine guns and numerous German strongpoints. Strongpoints such as Potsdam, Vampire, Gallipoli, Somme and Borry Farms inflicted appalling casualties on the attackers, and it was clear that the progress on this part of the front would be minimal.

However, XVIII Corps was managing to make better headway towards its objectives. Although the German resistance was strong, the corps nevertheless managed to push forward through stubborn strongpoints and obstacles to capture Border House, St Julien, Maison du Hibou and Hillock Farm, shifting the British front line well in front of the Steenbeek. The corps also managed to hang on to its gains, deflecting several German counter-attacks.

Some significant gains were also made by XIV Corps during this violent day. The 20th Division drove on through its first two objective lines, taking Langemarck in the process, and then captured the Rat House and the White House. The left brigade of the attack also took Au Bon Gite, a concrete blockhouse that presented an unnerving challenge for the attackers. One 2nd Lieutenant H.W.H. Willes, King's Own Yorkshire Light Infantry, diarised the events of the day, and later reflected on the attack on this feature:

The capture of Au Bon Gite seemed well-nigh impossible; the general advance went on regardless of it, and it was perhaps this fact that upset the calculations of the enemy and caused him to surrender an hour after the attack had been launch. Captain Slade and his company of the 11th RB, with the aid of a smoke barrage, succeeded in getting under the walls, and, after much discussion, the defenders agreed to surrender, when thirty-two Germans were made prisoners …

H.W.H. Willes, Diary.

The capture of Au Bon Gite illustrates how effective coordination between artillery and infantry could pay dividends when tackling German strongpoints, here through the precision use of smoke barrages. Yet, implicit in this account is the fact that although the strongpoint contained fewer than forty Germans, it probably delayed the advance of an entire battalion for at least an hour. Repeat this story across the front, and we can see why the German defence in depth imposed such grindingly slow progress upon the Allies, especially when combined with poor terrain conditions.

Nevertheless, XIV Corps was generally successful in achieving all of its goals for the day. As well as the divisions cited above, the 29th Division, which included the Newfoundland Regiment, took its major objectives, including its portions of the Wilhelm Line, and then managed to drive off German counter-attacks in the late afternoon.

Such resilience in the face of German counter-attacks, however, was not repeated in many other areas of the front, which came in for concerted efforts by the Germans to reclaim lost territory. In the II Corps area, the German 34th Division attacked 169th Brigade at around 0700 hrs, moving forward with assault troops and artillery support. (The German artillery was becoming increasingly skilful at boxing the British troops off from resupply and reinforcements.) The vigour of the attack on exhausted British soldiers resulted in the brigade pulling back to its start line, this withdrawal having a similar knock-on effect on neighbouring formations.

The 8th Division was attacked at 0930 hrs and once again in the afternoon. Poor weather and a lack of effective forward observation meant that the division was unable to draw on the artillery support that might have saved the situation, and so it too was pushed back virtually to its start line by the end of the day. The 16th and 36th Divisions in XIX Corps experienced their own counter-attack at 0900 hrs. The German assault ran like a steamroller over the frontal British positions, and a terrified flight back to the start line began. The situation was so serious and chaotic that at one point British artillery was deliberately brought down on positions just in front of the start line to hold back the Germans, despite many British troops still being forward.

It must be acknowledged that the British forces were not the only ones involved with the battles around Langemarck. To the far north, the French were also delivering assaults on major series of fortified positions, including the formidable *Die Grachten* ('Three Canals') bridgehead on the Yser Canal. Fortunately for the French in this area, the inundated ground meant that most of the German ferro-concrete positions were built well above ground, hence they received the attention of devastating artillery bombardments that reduced many strongpoints to rubble. Thus the French were able to advance and capture all their objectives for the day. The tortuous ground over which the French had to cross meant that the Germans found it hard to counter-attack in these areas, allowing the French to hang onto their gains.

DID YOU KNOW?

Trench foot was endemic to Third Ypres. It was a necrotising infection of the feet caused by damp and insanitary conditions. If not treated, it could lead to gangrene, necessitating amputation of the foot or toes.

The Battle of Langemarck rumbled on for two more days, but by the 17th it was clear that overall the operation had not yielded significant results for the British. General Gough admitted that the results had been uneven, with II Corps facing greater issues in terms of adverse terrain, artillery fire and counter-attacks, when compared to the progress of XIV and XVIII Corps. He also felt that some British units could have better resisted the German assaults in order to hold onto their gains. Haig, however, did his own fact-finding and came to some different conclusions when speaking to commanders of XIX Corps:

> But I gather that the attacking troops had a long march up the evening before the battle through Ypres to the front line and then had to fight from zero 4.45 a.m. until nightfall. The men could have had no sleep and must have been dead tired. Here also a number of concrete buildings and dugouts were never really destroyed by artillery fire, and do not appear to have been taken. So the advances made here were small …
>
> The cause of the failure to advance on the right centre of the attack of the Fifth Army is due, I think, to commanders being in too great a hurry! Three more days should have been allowed in which, if fine, the artillery would have dominated the enemy's artillery, and destroyed the concrete defences! After Gough has got the facts more fully I have arranged to talk the matter over with him.
>
> Haig, August 1917.

Haig's analysis is a mixed affair. On the one hand he recognises, with justification, the role that fatigue may have played in the setbacks of the day, the sleep-deprived men being unable to maintain the momentum of the attack, nor consolidate their positions against the German counter-attacks. At the same time he also blames the impetuousness of the officer class, for launching an offensive too early when artillery might have done their job for them.

Of course, much is to be attributed to hindsight here. While more rest and a longer preparatory bombardment might have made a difference in some sectors, whether these measures would have tipped the balance of the battle is far from certain. Yet while the attack on the 16th was largely a failure, we must not imagine that the Germans were the victors. By this stage of the battle, the Fourth Army had suffered terrible attrition amongst its front-line units, and every defence and counter-attack depleted the available manpower still further. Percival Phillips had an insight into the nature of the British enemy during his reporting on the battle:

> I talked today with a number of wounded men engaged in the fighting in Langemarck and beyond, and they are unanimous in declaring that the enemy infantry made a very poor show wherever they were deprived of their supporting machine guns and forced to choose between meeting a bayonet charge and fight. The mud was our men's greatest grievance. It clung to their legs at every step. Frequently they had to pause to pull their comrades from the treacherous mire – figures embedded to the waist, some of them trying to fire their rifles at a spitting machine gun and yet, despite these almost incredible difficulties, they saved each other and fought the Hun through the floods to Langemarck.
>
> Phillips, *Daily Express*, 17 August 1917.

The fact that the Germans were so effective in the counter-attack means that we have to take Phillip's low impression of German fighting spirit with a pinch of salt. It was nonetheless true that the German defence in depth depended heavily on large numbers of machine guns delivering interlocking fire across the front. Through this means, and intelligently positioned strongpoints, the German Army was well able to compensate for the lack of experience and training in some quarters of the army.

Whatever the reasons for the failure, the fact was that the battle had not brought the resolution the British hoped for. Furthermore, the fighting rippled on across the front throughout August, as local forces jostled over strongpoints and features already soaked in blood. These actions, too numerous to describe here in detail, resulted in few major adjustments in the front line. The biggest of the attacks took place on 22 August. Gough later explained the objectives and results of this push:

> On 22 August another general attack was made by the three corps on the right – the II, XIX and XVIII. The objectives in this attack had been reduced to those within a short distance of our line, as it was impossible for the men to go forward over any long distance; my object was to spare the troops to the utmost possible degree, while at the same time complying with my order from GHQ to the effect that the battle must be continued.
>
> The II Corps as usual met with a violent opposition, and counter-attacks were launched against its 14th Division which continued during 23 and 24 August, and involved very heavy fighting.
>
> Hubert Gough, *The Fifth Army* (London: Hodder & Stoughton, 1931) p.238.

What they did do, however, was rack up the body count. Between 16 and 28 August, the Allied casualties numbered just over 36,000, while the Germans took between 24,000 and 30,000 losses. This was despite the fact that from 14–31 August, with one or two days of exception, the weather was largely dry and hot. This fact brought challenges of its own. Landscapes that had been torn up by shell and mud hardened into rough landscapes that were difficult to cross by men, vehicles and horses. Yet, at the end of the month the rainclouds gathered once more, and the landscape began to dissolve again. Both sides licked their wounds and waited for the next development.

DID YOU KNOW?

The risks of drowning in liquid mud were increased by the loads soldiers carried. A British soldier in full kit could have a burden of 80lb (36kg) wrapped around his torso, making it especially difficult to escape when floundering in mud.

Timeline

1917

10 August		Battle of Westhoek. British forces launch an attack against the Gheluvelt Plateau, Westhoek itself is occupied, but either side of the village the British only manage advances of around 450 yards (411m)
11 August		18th Division loses a pillbox to a German counter-attack, but recaptures it by 0600 hrs
16 August		The Fifth Army launches, at 0445 hrs, a new attack against the Gheluvelt Plateau. Although a 1,500 yard (1,372m) advance is made in the north, most of the other assaults run to a stop, then German counter-attacks force a widespread British withdrawal

Strategic Focus

So far, the Battle of Third Ypres had fallen short of almost all the major strategic objectives Haig had outlined for the Flanders campaign early in 1917. Tens of thousands of lives had been expended, and many of the Allied gains had been overturned by German counter-attacks. Haig naturally came under questioning regarding the value of continuing the campaign.

In classic fashion, Haig remained resolute. On 21 August he delivered a report to the War Office, which contained the following declaration:

If we are favoured with a fine autumn … I regard the prospects of clearing the coast before winter sets in as still very hopeful, notwithstanding the loss of time caused by the bad weather during the first half of August. At the least, I see no reason to doubt that we shall be able to gain positions from which subsequent operations to clear the coast will present a far easier problem than we had to cope with at the outset of this offensive, and in which the losses and hardships suffered around Ypres in previous winters will be much reduced. In these circumstances the right course to pursue, in my opinion, is undoubtedly to continue to press the enemy in Flanders without intermission and to the full extent of our powers, and if complete success is not gained before the winter sets in, to renew the attack at the earliest possible moment next year. Success in clearing the coast may confidently be expected to have such strategical and political effects that they are likely to prove decisive.

Haig, 21 August 1917.

In essence, Haig was simply saying 'press on' and wear the enemy down. The devil was largely in the statement 'If we are favoured with a good autumn …' As August, the peak summer month, had seen very heavy rainfall, making further progress conditional on good autumn weather seemed in many ways like an exercise in wishful thinking. Furthermore, the very next day Haig postponed indefinitely the prospect of an amphibious landing near Ostend, following consultations with General Rawlinson (lieutenant-general of the Fourth Army) and Admiral Reginald Bacon (commander of the Dover Patrol). This decision rather kicked the legs from beneath his declarations that the Belgian coast could be taken.

At the same time, Haig began to make adjustments in the command relationships at Ypres. He was starting to tire of Gough's efforts, and an immediate goal was for the British to push forward through Zandvoorde and capture Polygon Wood and the ridge beyond. To accomplish this, Haig extended the left flank of the Second Army to the Ypres–Roulers railway, with the main

objectives for the army being the capture of the Broodseinde–
Polygon Wood ridge. The command effect of this decision was,
by handing over the II Corps front to the Second Army, to place
Plumer at the centre of the operation at Passchendaele. Gough
was now side-lined, and the focus of the action was now in the
hands of Plumer. It would prove to be an onerous commitment.

Menin Road Ridge and Polygon Wood

The first three weeks of September were relatively quiet on
the Flanders front. This is not to say that there were no locally
significant actions. Numerous minor attacks were launched
by both sides, particularly by the British as they tried to acquire
tactically significant scraps of land that had eluded them thus
far. On 4 September, for example, the 2/8th Warwicks of the
182nd Brigade, 61st Division, made an attack on Aisne Farm. The
Germans resisted with now-customary tenacity, and although
the British got within 30 yards (27m) of their objective, they were
pushed back again with heavy losses. Conversely, on 9 September
the Germans in II Corps' sector attacked around Inverness Copse,
but this time it was the British defence that held.

*Exhausted British troops slump down after the Battle of the Menin Road
Ridge, an action that cost more than 20,000 British casualties.*

Such actions continued on an almost daily basis, but Plumer had bigger plans developing. He brought with him a different tactical perspective to the Battle of Ypres. Gough, with the endorsement of Haig, had sought big results across a broad front. Plumer, by contrast, had more of a 'bite and hold' perspective. He intended to further the British gains at Ypres through a more focused sequence of attacks, each across a narrower front but with overwhelming infantry power and artillery support. The depth of each attack would be shallower, enabling the infantry to push forward quickly then consolidate their gains in expectation of the inevitable German counter-attacks.

By digging in sooner, the British could enjoy the advantages of a solid defence, allowing the German *Eingreif* divisions to break themselves on the British positions. Furthermore, Plumer massively increased the weight of artillery that would now operate in support. By pulling in large numbers of medium and heavy field guns from VII Corps plus the Third and Fourth Armies in northern France, Plumer gathered his guns in front of the Gheluvelt Plateau in a density to about one gun for every 5ft (1.5m) of front. Using such firepower, he hoped to deliver creeping barrages of irresistible intensity, and establish counter-battery responses that would suppress the Germans' own artillery. Note that the British were, by this time, thoroughly comfortable with using poison gas in their own methods of making war. Gas shells proved to be grimly effective not only in breaking up the coherence of German infantry units, but also of nullifying enemy artillery teams – it is hard to operate a heavy gun properly when surrounded by clouds of choking gas, even if the soldier is wearing a gas mask.

The focus of Plumer's efforts in September would be the Gheluvelt Plateau, and shelling of the German defences in this region began steadily from 31 August – it would build up to a stunning crescendo for the attack date, scheduled for 25 September. Plumer rearranged the corps for the attack. X Corps and I ANZAC Corps took over the positions previously occupied by II Corps, and V Corps also replaced XIX Corps. The overall

Horses remained the main form of motive power for the British and German forces in the First World War; hundreds of thousands were lost to bullet, shell and exhaustion.

attack would take place over an 8-mile (13km) front, although the strike at the Gheluvelt Plateau itself would be undertaken across a 4,000-yard (3,658m) front by the 41st and 23rd Divisions (X Corps) and the 1st and 2nd Australian Divisions (I ANZAC Corps).

Key objectives of the strike here would be positions now familiar to most British soldiers: Nonne Bosschen, Glencorse Wood, Inverness Copse, Polygon Wood and Tower Hamlets. In the official history of the campaign, Brigadier General Sir James Edmonds explained how Plumer had fine-tuned the battle plan:

General Plumer's intention was to capture the plateau by four separate steps, with an interval of six days between each to allow time to bring forward artillery and supplies; the distance of each step, governed by the need to meet the strong German counter-attacks with fresh infantry supported by an effective artillery barrage, was to be limited to about fifteen hundred yards. For the first step he considered a thousand yards to be the maximum frontage for each division.

James E. Edmonds, *Military Operations. France and Belgium, 1917*, Volume II (London: HMSO, 1948) p.237.

Note that each penetration would only be a matter of about 1,500 yards (1,372m) before the British soldiers consolidated the ground for a defence. Plumer was going to take his time, and hopefully avoid the terribly wasteful offensive strategies applied in the previous two months. The Fifth Army would by no means be idle during the assault on Gheluvelt Plateau. They would attack simultaneously on the Passchendaele–Staden Ridge, facing their own set of dire challenges and edging towards a place that would became synonymous with the battle in its entirety.

The offensive, known to history as the Battle of the Menin Road Ridge, began at 0540 hrs on 20 September, with an artillery

Logistics became a major challenge of the Ypres campaign in 1917. The off-road landscape was nearly impossible to traverse, so the Allied road network became choked with traffic night and day.

barrage that seemed to augur the end of the world, even though it was controlled with considerable precision. The British guns were using improved fuse systems in many of their shells, which caused the munitions to explode almost immediately the shell nose touched the ground, resulted in less cratering for the advancing troops to negotiate and an intense blast effect on the recipients.

Following in the wake of the creeping barrage came the British troops, the officers and NCOs restraining them to prevent their running forward into the storm of shells. Unlike days past, the infantry were now working in small assault teams, moving quickly between the craters and into the opposing trenches, which they neutralised with a mix of rifle and machine-gun fire and liberal use of hand and rifle grenades.

The first day of the offensive, delivered by a total of 65,000 British and Commonwealth troops, was a stunning success. The Fifth Army managed to make advances of 1,000 yards (914m) by midday, while the Second Army pushed forward 1,500 yards (1,372m) and established itself securely on the Gheluvelt Plateau. Gough himself later noted:

> As usual in this battle, the Germans counter-attacked fiercely. On the V Corps front they launch no less than six counter-attacks. These were either beaten off, or our supporting troops immediately counter-attacked in their turn and once more drove the Germans out. Their losses were very heavy and we captured more than 1,300 prisoners. By the end of the day we had captured all our objectives with the exception of two farms – an average penetration of 1,000 yards along the front of attack.
>
> Gough, *The Fifth Army*, p.262.

This is not to say the day was without cost. In many sectors, the casualties were appalling on both sides, and some strongpoints resisted being taken with fanatical intensity. The 41st Division, for example, paid a terrible price to try (unsuccessfully) to suppress the network of pillboxes and blockhouses that constituted Tower Hamlets.

Yet for Haig, the day was positive proof of a new British Army tactic, advancing in small, powerful steps that destabilised the German tactic of elastic defence. Further proof of the soundness of this strategy seemed to come over the next few days. The German forces, infuriated by their losses, launched a succession of counter-attacks. Each was beaten back, but one of the biggest, and most threatening, came on 25 September when the Germans assaulted in force south of Polygon Wood. The attack arrived at a bad moment, when the 23rd Division of X Corps was being relieved by the 33rd Division. The British managed, just, to fight off the attack, but the losses to the 98th Brigade seriously weakened the formation and the role it would play in subsequent actions.

In fact, although the period 20–25 September was an Allied victory, it came at a price – total British casualties were 20,441, showing that with success came attrition.

Even as the Germans were counter-attacking, the victorious Plumer was planning the next stage of the attack, scheduled for 26 September. This would consist of a push to secure, at last, Polygon Wood, requiring an advance of another 1,200 yards (1,097m) into German-occupied territory. Polygon Wood itself would be the objective of I ANZAC Corps while the Fifth Army drove its 3rd and 59th Divisions towards Zonnebeke and Hill 40.

The attack was launched at 0550 hrs on the morning of the 26th, with the customary heavy barrage from the British guns. Fresh Allied troops were now in the mix, including the 33rd Division (relief for the 23rd Division) and the 5th and 4th Australian Divisions (relief for the 1st and 2nd Australian Divisions). The total frontage of the attack was about 5,000 yards (4,572m), and the British troops once again set out across a landscape strewn with bodies.

As well as the heavy German resistance, the churned-up landscape made the going extremely hard, and it was problematic moving the field guns forward until improvised paths had been laid across the craters and trenches. The ANZAC troops required almost continual artillery support for the duration of the day to make progress, making the demands on ammunition logistics extremely heavy.

Mounted troops move along the Ypres Road towards Polygon Wood. The attack on the wood on 26–27 September was one the more successful British drives of the whole offensive.

A 15in howitzer in action at Polygon Wood, 25 September 1917. The I ANZAC Corps used more than 200 such guns during the battle of late September.

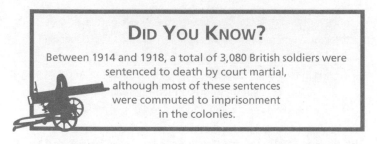

DID YOU KNOW?

Between 1914 and 1918, a total of 3,080 British soldiers were sentenced to death by court martial, although most of these sentences were commuted to imprisonment in the colonies.

The attack on the 26th was not without its problems. Ground fog and the smoke of the shelling made visibility poor in many locations, meaning that the attackers had to feel their way into appallingly heavy defensive fire. Certain German obstacles were not relinquished – the obdurate Tower Hamlets, for example, repelled the 39th Division. Yet in general, the attack was another vindication of Plumer's strategy, as most of the key objectives were taken (including Polygon Wood), albeit at the cost of another 15,375 men. German counter-attacks in most cases couldn't shake the British forces free, and morale amongst the German Fourth Army dropped to a new low.

The Germans were not passive, it should be noted, but the high command constantly wrestled with tactical solutions to the British advances. Ludendorff later remarked of this time:

After each attack I discussed the tactical experiences with General von Kuhl and Colonel von Lossberg, sometimes at the front, sometimes on the telephone ... Our defensive tactics had to be developed further, somehow or other ... The proposals of the officers on the spot tended rather in the direction of our former tactics; they amounted to a slight, but only slight, reinforcement of our front lines, and the abandonment of the counter-attack by the counter-attack divisions, local counter-attacks being substituted for this. These local counter-attacks were to be made by a division in the second line, to be brought close up and spread over a wide front, before the enemy's attack began. So, while the front was to be held rather more densely once more, in order to gain power, the whole battlefield was to be given more depth than ever. GH! Would thus, generally speaking, have to provide a second division for every fighting division in the front line, an unheard-of expenditure of force.

Ludendorff, quoted in John Terraine, *The Road to Passchendaele* (London: Leo Cooper, 1971) p.279.

The tension in Ludendorff's description here is palpable. The German forces needed increased manpower to make more rapid counter-attacks before the British could consolidate and further their offensive stride. Implicit in the last sentence here, however, is the suggestion of massive human waste. Between 21 and 30 September, the German Fourth Army had taken more than 13,000 casualties, and its manpower would be stretched to the limit. Fortunately for the Germans, they would soon have a meteorological ally.

Timeline

31 August British artillery begins to intensify shelling of Gheluvelt Plateau, in preparation for an offensive

20 September Battle of Menin Road Ridge begins, at 0540 hrs. British make advances of up to 1,500 yards (1,372m) and establish themselves on Gheluvelt Plateau

25 September Major German counter-attack around Polygon Wood, only just beaten back by the 98th Brigade

26 September Further British attack is launched to secure Polygon Wood, Zonnebeke and Hill 40. The attack managed to secure most of the key objectives, including Polygon Wood

1917

Broodseinde and Poelcappelle

It now appeared that the British momentum was unstoppable. Immediately another offensive action was planned on the Flanders front, scheduled for 4 October. It should be pointed out that September had been kind to the British forces in terms of the weather. There had been many fine and dry days, and the ground was therefore better suited to effective movement. Capitalising on this favourable climate, Plumer next aimed to push forward and take the remainder of the Gheluvelt Plateau and the Broodseinde Ridge.

What is noticeable about the battles of the Third Ypres in September and October is the increasingly central role that ANZAC forces were playing in the campaign. The Battle of Broodseinde, as it is known, was no exception. The 1st and 2nd Australian Divisions of I ANZAC Corps would take the brunt of capturing the Broodseinde Ridge, while the 3rd Australian Division and the New Zealand Division of II Anzac Corps had to tackle the well-defended Zonnebeke and Gravenstafel spurs.

Eight British divisions were also involved in the offensive, which began at 0600 hrs on 4 October. It had actually been planned for the 6th, but Haig was becoming increasingly concerned about the approach of adverse weather. Even with this precaution, the Allied forces suffered heavy rainfall during the night before the battle, and the battlefield was starting to get waterlogged again. In spite of this, the attack yet again was encouraging for the high command, although extremely violent and bloody for those who were delivering it. The soldiers of I ANZAC Corps, for example, met advancing German troops in no-man's-land, and the result was dreadful close-quarters combat, with bayonets being applied in earnest.

However, the Australian and New Zealand troops pressed on, and had taken the top of Broodseinde Ridge and Zonnebeke by 0900 hrs. X Corps, on the right of the attack, made good progress up the Gheluvelt Plateau, pushing forward another 1,500 yards

(1,372m) into enemy territory. The official military history later noted that:

> The two Brigades of the 7th Division, though short of their final objective now overlooked the broad Heulebeek depression between the plateau and the Keiberg spur to the north-east, and saw deep into the German back area in the Flemish lowlands towards Dadizeele.
>
> Edmonds, *Military Operations*, p.312.

In many places the Fifth Army pushed forward another 1,500 yards (1,372m), with the 11th Division inching towards Poelcappelle, aided by ten tanks of D Battalion, I Tank Brigade, which were put to good use neutralising pillboxes.

Broodseinde was another success, and the Germans had incurred many thousands of further casualties without being able to stop the Allied waves. But the action had also cost 20,000 British and Commonwealth dead and wounded. Plus, the rains

Canadian pioneers lay tape across the front line at Passchendaele, marking out the route for the laying of a corduroy road.

were starting to come in earnest, and the previously hard ground was now starting to suck at boots, wheels and hooves. With the men exhausted, and the conditions worsening, now was the point at which Haig could potentially call a halt to the offensive.

The fact that he did not has been held by historians as a singular black mark over his career. As ever, the analysis reveals shades of grey rather than black and white. The Russian exit from the war meant that now more German divisions would be available from the east; it could therefore be argued that the attack needed to keep its momentum before the German forces in the west could strengthen themselves. There was also clear evidence that the German morale was at breaking point in many sectors, therefore another 'push' could bring the final victory. Yet the Allied men were also shattered, and the weather conditions would act as a brake on the extent of advances. Lieutenant General Sir William Birdwood, commander of I ANZAC Corps, probably best sums up the ambiguities:

> My men were weak and tired, and when Plumer consulted me I had to advise against any further advance. However, since only one division of my Corps was to be involved in the next stage, and since the other Corps Commanders were in favour of pushing on, Haig decided to do so.
>
> In a sense, I was reminded of our final effort to capture Sari Bair at Gallipoli, for here again it was a case of 'so near and yet so far'. Haig's view was that if we held the main Passchendaele Ridge overlooking and commanding all the country to the east, this would involve so decisive a break in the German line that our cavalry could be used to good effect; and there is little doubt that if the weather had held, and if we had been able to prepare and rehearse our advance as carefully as in the first three stages, we should have been able to take Passchendaele. But the weather defeated us.
>
> Field Marshal Lord Birdwood, *Khaki and Gown: An Autobiography* (London: Ward Lock, 1942) p.316.

Birdwood recognised the 'what ifs' of warfare, and bluntly ascribed defeat to the effects of the weather. Haig was, nevertheless, not to be stopped whatever the weather was doing. For the next offensive, the Second Army was to make further strikes against key objectives, the most important of which was Passchendaele Ridge, the focus of the 49th and 66th Divisions of II ANZAC Corps.

Two British divisions – 66th (2nd East Lancashire) Division and 49th (West Riding) Division – had also been added as support for this attack, although the former was an extremely 'green' formation. To the north, XVIII Corps of Fifth Army was to send the 48th and 11th Divisions up the Passchendaele spur, while XIV Corps (4th, 29th and the Guards Divisions) advanced along the Ypres–Staden railway east of Poelcappelle. The French would also provide infantry support to the Fifth Army's northern flank.

The Battle of Poelcappelle was launched at 0520 hrs on 9 October. The contrast to the previous battles could not have been starker, or more ghastly. Just deploying to the front line

Royal Engineers bring up spools of telephone wire during the Battle of Poelcappelle. Laying the wires between front-line communication posts and headquarters was a perilous, exposed job.

through the driving rain and mud had exhausted many of the troops. The crushing artillery barrage that had been so effective in previous campaigns was now lacklustre. Many of the guns could not be brought into range across the glutinous landscape, or were emplaced on shifting platforms in the mud that made accurate shooting nigh-on impossible. The British Army's *Official History* of the campaign explains these problems in more detail:

> The field batteries of the II Anzac Corps which were to have been near the Zonnebeke–Winniped road to support the main attack had to remain west of the Steenbeek on hurriedly constructed and unstable gun-platforms. Until these were made many of the guns were up to their axles in mud, and some even to the muzzles. [Footnote: Each gun-platform had to have a foundation of fascines and road metal, on which was placed a double-decked platform of breech-slabs nailed together. It required two days' hard work to make, and a temporary plank road had to be built from the platform to the main roadway for the ammunition supply by pack transport. Even after this labour, many of the platforms began to sink into the mud after a few rounds had been fired.]
>
> *History of the Great War based on official documents by direction of the Historical Section of the Committee of Imperial Defence. Military Operations. France and Belgium, 1917: [Vol. II] Messines and Third Ypres (Passchendaele) 7 June – 10 November,* compiled and edited by Brigadier General Sir James E. Edmonds (London: HMSO, 1948), pp.327–28.

German batteries, such as those 7,000 yards (6,400m) behind the Passchendaele front line, could therefore deliver heavy salvos onto British troops as they advanced, while enjoying being beyond the range of counter-battery fire. Aerial observation, which had become so critical to the British artillery fire, was now either grounded or rendered ineffective by the weather. Those shells that were fired often buried themselves deep in the slick mud before exploding, losing much of their explosive power in the process.

A bleak image of the morning after a battle at Passchendaele. The terrible ground conditions made tactical infantry manoeuvres almost impossible.

The result was that the British soldiers struggled into the attack at a sluggish pace, exhausted, soaked through, and into the face of blistering German firepower. In many cases, the troops were stopped within a few hundred yards of advance and eventually forced back to their start positions, leaving the dead and wounded to be absorbed by the mud of the battlefield. The best progress was made by the 66th Division of II ANZAC Corps, which took and held onto its red line objectives. Yet by the end of the day, none of the major objectives had been taken, and 7,000 additional Allied casualties had been suffered.

Timeline

1917		
	4 October	The Battle of Broodseinde. ANZAC troops assault the Broodseinde Ridge
		Zonnebeke and Gravenstafel spurs, taking most their objective in just a few hours of assault
	5–8 October	Localised battles continue, including at Burns House, Vacher Farm and Celtic Wood
	9 October	The Battle of Poelcappelle. A British assault towards Passchendaele Ridge and Poelcappelle ends in muddy failure

The Experience of Battle

The Battle of Poelcappelle was, in essence, the beginning of the offensive drive towards Passchendaele itself (although what are officially known as the First and Second Battles for Passchendaele are yet to be described). While we can draw the broad outlines of strategies and tactics, we must also bore down deeper into what it meant to fight in Flanders during that terrible autumn and early winter of 1917.

One point to grasp immediately is that although the text here continually refers to specific features in the landscape, such as woods and villages, in many cases these were almost scarcely discernible, rubbed from the face of the earth by shell and bullet. Photos of Polygon Wood, for example, show little more than a few bare trunks sticking out of a denuded mud field. Villages could be indicated by slight variations in the type and quality of rubble strewn about the battlefield.

Then there was the mud. It is difficult to exaggerate the terrible quality of the mud at the Battle of Passchendaele. Men, even horses, drowned in bottomless shell holes. Placing one's foot in a puddle might suddenly result in dropping up to your armpits in mud, which then held you in a concrete-like grasp. Some men spent days like this, immobile until they either died or were rescued. The mud made every step a sucking ordeal, and keeping weapons and equipment functional in such conditions – let alone lugging it around – was nearly impossible. Fungal skin conditions and trench foot flourished.

Philip Gibbs, a journalist who later wrote a book about the battle entitled *Adventures in Journalism*, explained more about the conditions:

> Every man of ours who fought on the way to Passchendaele agreed that those battles in Flanders were the most awful, the most bloody, and the most hellish. The condition of the ground, out from Ypres and beyond the Menin Gate, was partly the

cause of the misery and the filth. Heavy rains fell, and made one great bog in which every shell crater was a deep pool. There were thousands of shell craters. Our guns had made them, and German gunfire, slashing our troops, made thousands more, linking them together so that they were like lakes in some places, filled with slimy water and dead bodies. Our infantry had to advance heavily laden with their kit, and with arms and hand-grenades and entrenching tools – like pack animals – along slimy duckboards on which it was hard to keep a footing, especially at night when the battalions were moved under cover of darkness.

You live for days in the closest contact with your comrades in a contracted space. You cannot move, and are unable to think clearly. Never did I realise how difficult it can be to lead a human life. There is nameless agony in it.

Philip Gibbs, *Adventures in Journalism* (London,: Heinemann, 1923), p.206.

The 'nameless agony' was reiterated by British playwright and novelist R.C. Sherriff, who fought at Passchendaele and was severely wounded there. Here he recounts what it was like to make an attack into those terrible conditions:

The order came to advance. There was no dramatic leap out of the trenches. The sandbags on the parapet were so slimy with rain and rotten with age that they fell apart when you tried to grip them. You had to crawl out through a slough of mud. Some of the older men, less athletic than the others, had to be heaved out bodily.

From then on, the whole thing became a drawn-out nightmare. There were no tree stumps or ruined buildings ahead to help you keep direction. The shelling had destroyed everything. As far as you could see, it was like an ocean of thick brown porridge. The wire entanglements had sunk into the mud, and frequently, when you went in up to the knees, your legs would come out with strands of barbed wire clinging to them, and your hands torn and bleeding through the struggle to drag them off ...

All this area had been desperately fought over in the earlier battles of Ypres. Many of the dead had been buried where they fell and the shells were unearthing and tossing up the decayed bodies. You would see them flying through the air and disintegrating ...

In the old German trench we came upon a long line of men, some lolling on the fire step, some sprawled on the ground, some standing upright, leaning against the trench wall. They were British soldiers – all dead or dying. Their medical officer had set up a first-aid station here, and these wounded men had crawled to the trench for his help. But the doctor and his orderlies had been killed by a shell that had wrecked his station, and the wounded men could only sit or lie there and die. There was no conceivable hope of carrying them away.

Robert Sherriff, *No Leading Lady* (London: Victor Gollancz Ltd, 1968), ebook.

The mud of Passchendaele. Falling into such craters while wearing full kit could result in an unfortunate soldier drowning, or at least being held fast.

Horses were not immune to the effects of the mud, as this haunting and famous image shows. If the animal was not freed quickly, it would be shot in situ.

Corduroy tracks were laid across the sodden Flanders battlefield to enable supplies to reach the front line. Here mules carry water supplies forward.

Trench digging could be a thankless task at Ypres, the trenches filling up quickly with both rainwater and ground water.

As the Ypres battle wore on, an ever-greater percentage of manpower effort was expended just on logistics and movement. Here we see a group of sappers forming a digging party.

What comes across in such an account is the sheer exhaustion of having to fight in these conditions, let alone simply move through them. For many soldiers, there came the dawning recognition that the time for victory had passed:

> 10 October. It was all out yesterday at the attack. It was the saddest day of this year. We did fairly well but only fairly well. It was not the enemy but mud that prevented us doing better. But there is now no chance of complete success here this year. We must still fight on for a few more weeks, but there is no purpose in it now, so far as Flanders is concerned … Moving up close behind a battle, when things are going well and when one is all keyed up with hope of great results, one passes without much thought the horrible part of it – the wounded coming back, the noise, the news of losses, the sight of men toiling through mud into great danger. But when one knows that the great purpose one has been working for has escaped, somehow one sees and thinks of nothing but the awfulness of it all.
>
> Brigadier General John Charteris, *At G.H.Q.* (London: Cassell, 1931) p.259.

The Battles of Passchendaele

So, despite the evidence before his eyes, Haig decided to press on. Now the main objective was Passchendaele. Formally a picturesque little Belgian village, it was now a devastated battlefield high point, situated some 150ft (46m) above sea level. Haig planned a new offensive to take this objective, set for 12 October.

Of course, the offensive had a neat linearity on paper. The honour of taking Passchendaele village itself was given to the 3rd Australian Division, while the New Zealand Division had to assault the Bellevue and Goudberg defences on the Wallemolen spur (both divisions were part of II ANZAC Corps). Meanwhile, on their right the 4th Australian Division, I ANZAC Corps, was to give flanking protection to the Passchendaele attack. To the left

Australian relief troops move up the front line. The ANZAC forces took the brunt of some of the later fighting in the Third Ypres campaign, during the push towards Passchendaele itself.

of II ANZAC Corps were five British divisions, which would also mount a supporting attack.

The seeds of disaster were sown from the start. The divisions involved in the Battle of Poelcappelle now had just two days to prepare for another offensive. This simply wasn't enough. The problems with emplacing artillery and bringing up ammunition had grown even more acute, thus the British would not have the requisite artillery support needed for an effective push. Another point of concern was that the ANZAC troops assaulting towards Passchendaele were reporting, before they even set off, that the Germans had emplaced very dense networks of barbed wire in front of their positions.

Furthermore, as the troops deployed forward to the jumping-off points for the offensive, they were shelled incessantly by the German artillery, taking heavy casualties even before battle. When they finally did attack, at 0525 hrs on the morning of 12 October, a human tragedy unfolded as Australian, New Zealand, Canadian and British troops began an unimaginable ordeal. The experience of the New Zealand Division is representative. The *Official History* notes:

> The artillery barrage intended to support the advance of the New Zealand Division, weak and erratic at the start, became even thinner and more ragged as the troops advanced up the slope, howitzer shells burying themselves in the sodden ground and merely splashing the pillboxes with fountains of mud. In consequence, the New Zealanders found themselves confronted with broad belts of unbroken barbed wire entanglements … This splendid division lost a hundred officers and 2,635 other ranks within a few hours in brave but vain attempts – its only failure – to carry out a task beyond the power of any infantry with so little support, and had gained no ground except on the left.
>
> Edmonds, *Official History*, pp.341–42.

The fact was that the physical conditions that now prevailed over Flanders were making meaningful offensive movement almost impossible, especially as the power of British artillery had been largely negated. The Australian divisions, like their New Zealand comrades, found themselves thrust into a battle that quickly lost all sense of coherence. The 9th Brigade of the 3rd Australian Division, for example, began the offensive under German shell fire, losing men on the very start line of the advance.

Nevertheless, the 35th Battalion managed to push on into Passchendaele village itself; they found it largely deserted, but by the time it reached there its strength was so depleted and its advance was so isolated that it pulled back almost to its start line. The 10th Australian Brigade, attacking south of the Ravebeek, had a similar experience, its ranks chopped to pieces by German enfilading fire.

The British fared no better. Many of the XVIII Corps' assaults came to a halt little more than 100 yards (91m) from their start lines. Some gains were made at the far north of the offensive, however. The 4th and 17th Divisions, advancing along the Ypres–Staden railway, made headway, with the 17th (Northern) Division taking all its objectives. The Guards Division also gave good account, moving up to the edge of the Houthulst Forest and taking the German strongpoints of Angle Point and Aden House.

On the whole, a day that began dreadfully for the Allies ended dreadfully. The high ground of Passchendaele Ridge remained in German hands, despite the Allies having taken a casualty toll of between 13,000 and 15,000 men, mostly for negligible physical gains on the battlefield.

But there was more bloodshed to come. Haig and a select group of others were convinced that the offensive had to be maintained, especially if decent weather could be obtained later in the month. In his diary entry of 13 October, by which time the First Battle of Passchendaele had stopped, Haig noted:

> The Army Commanders explained the situation; all agreed that mud and the bad weather prevented our troops getting on yesterday. I said that the immediate objective was the mass of high ground about Passchendaele. Once this was taken the rest of the ridge would fall more easily. The Canadians would join Second Army at once … The enemy seems to have increased the number of his machine guns in front. This necessitates a larger bombardment. We all agreed that our attack should only be launched when there is a fair prospect of fine weather. *When the ground is dry* no opposition which the enemy has put up has been able to stop our men. The ground is so soft in places, the D.G.T. (Nash) told us, that he has light engines on the 60cm railways sunk up the boilers in mud. The track has completely disappeared.
>
> Haig, Diary, 13 October 1917.

Haig's diary makes it clear that he was far from dismissive of the weather conditions, and their effect over the battlefield. Nor were his protestations of the German Fourth Army being virtually on its knees entirely inaccurate. Documents written by Ludendorff show a real concern that Germany was becoming scarcely capable of providing replacements and reinforcements to the Fourth Army (between 1 July and 10 October 1917, the German forces at Flanders had lost an estimated 159,000 men). General von Kuhl even proposed a strategic withdrawal in a conference on 18 October, although this proposition was vigorously rejected by von Arnim and his chief of staff, who argued that yielding any ground would give the Allies an advantage of movement and risk German losing its critical U-boat bases on the Western European coastlines.

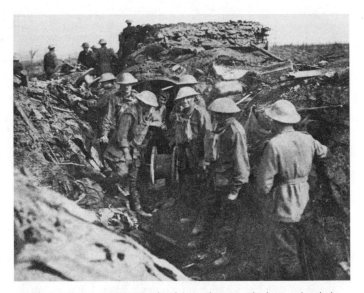

An observation post near Westhoek; we also see telephone wires being laid. Keeping communications open across a devastated battlefield was a fundamental problem of all First World War campaigns.

A British telephone exchange, perilously situated within 500 yards of the German lines, transmits orders from forward observation officers to the artillery batteries to the rear.

A telephonist receives range information for his artillery battery. The First World War saw huge advances in the accurate delivery of indirect fire, making creeping barrages feasible.

So, for now, the Germans would keep resisting and the British would keep attacking. Haig was also eager to keep up the Flanders offensive to resist French requests that the British extend their line, and take over more responsibility on the Western Front. Haig was against dissipating his forces, and he was also aware that the more he could wear down the German forces in Flanders, the better the starting point for the British offensive at Cambrai further south, planned for November.

To make the next push at Passchendaele more effective (hopefully), Haig replaced the battle-weary II ANZAC Corps with the four divisions of the Canadian Corps on 17/18 October. This corps was commanded by Lieutenant General Sir A.W. Currie, a true combat leader who had a good relationship and similar combat philosophy to Plumer. Currie, like Plumer, favoured a series of short, vigorous and progressive offensive steps, strongly supported by artillery, as the way to surmount the Passchendaele Ridge and take up effective defensive positions for the winter months. He also focused on improving the logistical flow of munitions, men and materiel to the front line, so the momentum of the attacks could achieve a better operational tempo.

The Second Battle of Passchendaele was launched on 26 October, although the British artillery was doing its preparatory work days before, focusing much effort on negating barbed-wire and pillboxes on the Wallemolen spur and Bellevue. The initial push was to be focused and concentrated. The 3rd and 4th Canadian Divisions were to attack around the flooded Ravebeek Valley towards Passchendaele village. In terms of flanking support, the left flank would be driven forward by the 63rd (Royal Naval) Division, the 58th (2/1st London) Division, the 57th (2nd West Lancashire) Division, the 50th (Northumbrian) Division and two French First Army divisions. To the right were the 7th and 5th Divisions of X Corps, making an attack against the Gheluvelt Plateau in the hope of distracting German focus away from the push towards Passchendaele.

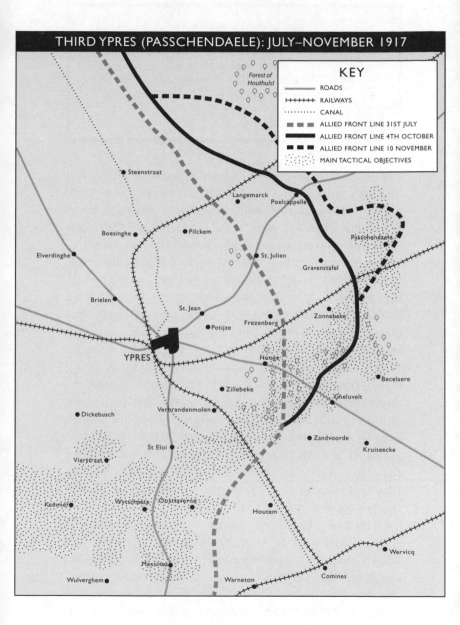

THIRD YPRES (PASSCHENDAELE): JULY–NOVEMBER 1917

KEY

ROADS	
+++++ RAILWAYS	
·········· CANAL	
▬ ▬ ▬ ALLIED FRONT LINE 31ST JULY	
▬▬▬ ALLIED FRONT LINE 4TH OCTOBER	
▪ ▪ ▪ ALLIED FRONT LINE 10 NOVEMBER	
∷∷ MAIN TACTICAL OBJECTIVES	

Forest of Houthulst

Steenstraat

Langemarck
Poelcappelle

Boesinghe
Pilckem
Passchendaele

Elverdinghe
St. Julien
Gravenstafel

Brielen
St. Jean
Zonnebeke

Potijze
Frezenberg

YPRES
Hooge
Becelaere

Zillebeke
Gheluvelt

Dickebusch
Verbrandenmolen
Zandvoorde
Kruiseecke

St Eloi

Vierstraat
Houtem

Kemmel
Wytschaete
Oosttaverne
Wervicq

Messines
Warneton
Comines

Wulverghem

DID YOU KNOW?

Not everyone was impressed with the French effort along the Aisne in 1917. Haig, in a letter to his wife on 24 October, noted bitterly: 'The French did well yesterday … If the French had only made this attack 6 weeks ago, it would have had a much more decisive effect.'

It should be noted that on 23 October the French forces had also begun a major offensive action along the Aisne further south. Known to the French as the Battle of Malmaison, the attack forced the Germans to retreat back across the Oise–Aisne Canal line, losing thousands of men and much equipment in the process.

Back at Passchendaele, the first day of battle for the British and Canadians brought fresh levels of torment to the men on the battlefield. The rain was still falling, at times heavily, but the artillery creeping barrage was delivered more efficiently than during the previous attack. The Canadian 4th Brigade, attacking along the Passchendaele Road beneath the Ravebeek, managed to drive in to its red line objectives, but the level of casualties was mounting at a terrifying rate. The 46th Battalion, for example, lost 70 per cent of its strength during that one day of fighting, and was forced to pull back to just near the Ravebeek. The 3rd Division, however, managed to clear the German strongpoints at Bellevue, Laamkeek and Wold Copse, although some formation were forced to pull back slightly from their gains to prevent exposing their flanks. Nevertheless by mid-afternoon the Canadians had largely made their first step towards Passchendaele.

On the flanks, by contrast, the operation was unravelling. The advances were minimal, while the losses were horrendous. Six Allied divisions assaulting on the flanks of the battle took combined casualties of 8,723 men, with many units ending up back at their start lines. The first 'step' of the attack on Passchendaele had been costly in the extreme, but the offensive was not to end yet. In fact, some finer weather broke mercifully through the clouds, a fact that aided the resupply for the next push. The Canadian supply trains made herculean efforts to get supplies through, hundreds of pack animals winding their ways across duckboard roads with drowning mud on both sides, and shelling a constant companion.

Despite the dangers and the physical obstacles, the British and Canadians were ready for the next push on 30 October. Stepping out after the now-customary storm of fire from the Allied artillery unleashed at 0550 hrs, the Canadians headed out to their objectives – a series of positions along the southern edge of Passchendaele, positions that would be perfect for the final step of taking the village itself. The Canadians showed epic levels of persistence in their attack. Despite some battalions (such as the 85th) losing 50 per cent of their strength in the assault, the Canadian forces nonetheless managed to push forward and take up positions on the outskirts of Passchendaele, overcoming strongpoints such as Vienna Cottage, Snipe Hall, Duck Lodge, Source Farm and Vapour Farm.

As the day progressed, an unwelcome visitor returned in the form of very heavy rain. The British divisions operating on the Canadians' left – 63rd (Royal Naval) and 58th (2/1st London) Divisions – again struggled to make any progress, advancing little more than 100 yards (91m) but taking hundreds of casualties, especially from German artillery barrages ranged in behind the British creeping barrage. The slippery mass of the inundated Lekkerboterbeek made every step forward a nightmare.

Regardless of the means or the cost, the fact remained that the Canadians were indeed stepping closer to taking Passchendaele itself. The final, major drive came on 6 November. The attack had been aided by three rainless days in the first week of November, which allowed the Allies to make adequate preparations and readjustments of their forces. XVIII Corps was replaced by II Corps; 2nd Canadian Division relieved 4th Canadian Division; the 1st Canadian Division relieved the 3rd Canadian Division; the 35th Division was replaced in the line by the 18th Division of

XIX Corps. Thus refreshed, the soldiers mounted the final assault against Passchendaele at 0600 hrs on 6 November. While the Canadians would have the central push against Passchendaele and Mosselmarkt (a position north-west of Passchendaele), the left flank would be driven by II Corps and the right flank by I ANZAC Corps.

Passchendaele village, an objective that had frequently seemed unobtainable during the previous months of fighting, at last fell to the Canadians. The 27th, 28th and 31st Divisions pushed into the largely deserted village within minutes of the launch of the offensive. Despite having to deal with some German resistance from pillboxes to the north of the village, the Canadians managed to secure the village and eastern positions on the ridge by 0900 hrs. Meanwhile the 1st Canadian Brigade, 1st Canadian Division accomplished their occupation of the Mosselmarkt blockhouse, the Germans within largely taken by surprise.

The morning of attack had gone relatively well for the Allies, but as the day wore on the rain grew heavier, the ground grew more impassable and the German counter-attacks grew stronger. Although the Allies managed to hang on to their gains, it was clear that no further progress was going to be made that day. The Battle of Third Ypres was now drawing to its close. A final drive forward was made on 10 November, the 1st Canadian Division going forward several hundred yards to occupy more of the main ridgeline, capturing the strongpoints of Venture Farm and Vindictive Crossroads.

Following this last gasp, Haig called the offensive to a close on 20 November. The Canadians, holding onto a precarious line composed of rain-filled craters and fragmented trench lines, must have reflected upon the cost of these gains – the Canadian Corps had lost 12,924 men since they arrived in Flanders.

Timeline

1917

12 October	First Battle of Passchendaele begins. In terrible weather, and with poor artillery support, ANZAC and British forces make few gains towards Passchendaele, but suffer 13,000 and 15,000 casualties
17/18 October	Four ANZAC divisions are relieved by the Canadian Corps
22 October	British forces apply pressure at Passchendaele with a four-division assault at key points of the line, although the gains are minimal
26 October	Second Battle of Passchendaele begins. The Canadians make progress towards Passchendaele, although some battalions lose up to 70 per cent of their strength
30 October	Another push towards Passchendaele brings promising results: the Canadians reach the outskirts of Passchendaele, and take strongpoints such as Vienna Cottage, Snipe Hall, Duck Lodge, Source Farm and Vapour Farm
6 November	An Allied attack on Passchendaele sees Passchendaele village and Mosselmarkt blockhouse taken by the Canadians, although heavy losses and terrible weather severely affect operations
10 November	The British and Canadian forces make one final push, capturing much of the Passchendaele ridge
20 November	The Third Ypres campaign is brought to a close

AFTER THE BATTLE

The Battle of Third Ypres, more popularly known as the Battle of Passchendaele, has come to represent what is seen as the ultimate futility of the tactics applied in the First World War. This view has much to recommend it. Even at the time of the offensive, there were many politicians and senior Allied commanders who questioned the merit of pushing forward. Some even had second thoughts about the value of the retaining the Ypres Salient in general, as we have seen.

Much of this questioning derives from a near exclusive focus on the British casualties, and the limits of British gains. Indeed, over the duration of the Ypres offensive, the Allied forces took some 250,000 casualties, pouring more than fifty divisions into the maelstrom for gains that at their maximum were no more than 5 miles (8km) deep.

Furthermore, the conditions in which men fought and died were dreadful beyond belief, especially once the rains set in. General Launcelot Kiggell, Haig's chief of staff, actually found tears in his eyes when he finally visited the front in the autumn and saw the conditions in front of him. 'Good God, did we really send men to fight in that?' he is said to have remarked, with emotion. Here, if anything, is the real guilt to be found in the Passchendaele offensive. Plumer was right to acknowledge that the major British successes were had during periods of fine weather. Armies must be prepared to fight in adverse weather, but sending attacks out across what was effectively an ocean of slime paid limited dividends in return for maximum bloodshed.

So why was the attack prosecuted over such as long period of time? To do full justice to that question, we need to look across no-man's-land to the German side. Flanders was, in many ways, a millstone around the neck of the German forces in the area, as much as it was for the British. The Germans couldn't withdraw from the area, for to do so would weaken their hold on the Belgian coastline and their ability to prosecute the U-boat war against the Allies. Furthermore, having a large chunk of Belgium in its possession ensured that Germany had more tools in the box for future peace negotiations. But the land itself was a nightmare to hold, General von Kuhl explained something of the nature of the challenge for the Germans:

> In the Flanders battle there were no trenches, no dug-outs. With ground water just below the surface it was not possible to drive tunnels into the soil … The defenders cowered in their water-filled craters without protection from the weather; hungry and freezing, completely without cover from continual artillery fire. Even the staffs of the forward unit had no cover, except perhaps a thin corrugated iron roof over the shell-hole. Movement in the muddy soil was very difficult and men and horses sank into the slime; rifles and machine guns, coated with mud, refused to function. Only rarely was it possible to supply the defenders with a hot meal. Distribution or orders in the forward area was difficult in the extreme as telephone and line communication had been shot to pieces. With difficulty runners made their way through the mud.
>
> Von Kuhl, quoted in Terraine, *Road to Passchendaele*, p.337.

Maintaining the Flanders front under these conditions was enormously costly for the Germans in terms of manpower, logistics and energy. In total, the Battle of Third Ypres consumed 200,000 of Germany's soldiers, so to say that the British offensive achieved nothing would be a short-sighted (albeit humane) statement. The memoirs of Ludendorff corroborate the strain of the German resistance at Flanders, and also broaden the reflections to tactical considerations:

> On the 31st of July the English, assisted by a few French Divisions on their left, had attacked on a front of about 31 kilometres, but besides the loss of from two to four kilometres along the whole front, it caused us very heavy losses in prisoners and stores, and a heavy expenditure of reserves.
>
> On the 16th we sustained another great blow. The English pressed on beyond Poelcappelle, and even with an extreme exertion of strength on our part, could only be pushed back a short distance. It had cost us heavily.
>
> The costly August battles imposed a heavy strain on the Western troops. In spite of all the concrete protection they seemed more or less powerless under the enormous weight of the enemy's artillery. At some points they no longer displayed that firmness which I in common with the local commanders had hoped for.
>
> The enemy managed to adapt himself to our method of employing counter-attack Divisions. There were no more attacks with unlimited objectives, such as General Nivelle had made in the Aisne-Champagne battle. He was ready for our counter-attacks and prepared for them by exercising restraint in the exploitation of success.
>
> I was myself being put to a terrible strain. The state of affairs in the West appeared to prevent the execution of our plans elsewhere. Our wastage had been so high as to cause grave misgivings and exceeded all expectation. The attack on the Dvina had to be postponed repeatedly. Indeed, it became a question whether we could continue to bear the responsibility of retaining those Divisions in the East.

> After a period of profound quiet in the West, which led some
> to hope that the battle of Flanders was over, another terrific
> assault was made on our lines on the 10th of September. The
> third bloody act of the battle had begun.
>
> Ludendorff, quoted in www.firstworldwar.com.

Several elements of this passage deserve our focus. The first is the genuine respect Ludendorff shows for the British artillery. The old days of crude, bludgeoning artillery barrages were gone, and now the British could make a coordinated match between infantry movement and artillery placement. It is evident that only when the weather conditions deteriorated significantly in the autumn, and artillery accuracy and volumes of fire were affected, the progress of the British ground attacks became even more painful. The critical passage here, however, is the acknowledgement that the British tactics were working, especially in terms of adapting to the German system of counter-attacks. By avoiding the 'unlimited objectives', and making short pushes forward with quick consolidations, the British undermined the entire German rationale of defence in depth.

So, if Third Ypres imposed terrible attrition on the German Army, kept the forces in Flanders pinned down, pioneered more effective assault tactics and refined the development of artillery control, then we should avoid classifying it as an unmitigated failure.

Yet, nor can it be classed as a victory. The biggest problem for Haig was that far from securing the Flanders front for the British, it actually made the front less easy to defend. The Ypres Salient had now broadened outwards, the front line a fragile crust of staggered and erratic positions, little more than loosely connected shell-holes. Defending this front, particularly with an army exhausted by the efforts of previous months, would not be easy. Haig himself raised this issue with the chief of the imperial general staff, Field Marshal Sir William Robertson, in a communication of 15 November:

DID YOU KNOW?

During the battle of Third Ypres, the British and Commonwealth troops captured 24,065 prisoners, 74 artillery pieces, 941 machine guns and 138 trench mortars.

The positions already gained on that [Flanders] front fall short of what I had wished to secure before the winter … Our present position … may be difficult and costly to hold if seriously attacked … I think this latter contingency must be expected as soon as the enemy realises that he has regained the initiative …

In view of the advanced season and existing state of the enemy's infantry on this front such attacks are, for the present, unlikely to aim at more than local and limited objectives on which a heavy concentration of hostile artillery can be brought to bear.

Haig, 15 November 1917.

Having given his all to prolonging the offensive, and frequently against the opposition of the highest levels of government, Haig here appears rather careworn and anxious. Most ominous is his statement that the Germans would eventually realise that they have 'regained the initiative', implying that the British were only temporarily in charge of the situation. Such a fear indeed had a prophetic edge.

The Offensives of 1918

The German spring offensives of 1918 couldn't have been a bigger shock to the Allies. The war was now four years old, millions of lives had been expended, but still the German Army was able to unleash a massive offensive across the Western Front that, for a time, even seemed to augur a German victory.

Using formations released from the Eastern Front, the German forces threw six armies against the Allies across the Western Front. The most powerful element of the St Michael Offensive, launched on 21 March, was conducted by the German Second, Seventh and Eighteenth Armies against the British Third and Fifth Armies on the Somme (Gough was still in charge of the redeployed Fifth Army).

Totally outclassed in firepower and manpower, the British Fifth and French Sixth Army (holding the line on the right flank of the British) were thrown into a chaotic retreat by a sequence of attacks, entire divisions being routed by the strength of the German firepower and assault. The greatest advances of that spring were made in the Somme sector, the line moving back around 40 miles (64km) closer to Paris. For the British, these were desperate times. In the first day of the offensive alone, the British forces lost 20,000 dead and 35,000 wounded.

Further north, in Flanders, the British would face the German offensive later, on 9 April, with the opening of Operation Georgette. After a two-day preparatory bombardment, which began on the 7th, twenty-six divisions of the German Sixth Army made the thrust towards Ypres. The overall, ambitious objective was to crush the Ypres Salient, capture Ypres itself, then drive on to the Belgian coast and cut off the British supply lines running from the ports of Calais, Dunkirk and Boulogne.

Plumer's Second Army was still holding the Flanders line, and it was pushed into a series of costly retreats. By 17 April, the British had abandoned the Passchendaele Ridge and the Messines Ridge was also back in German hands. The ground that had been won with so much blood the previous year was retaken, proving Haig's concerns about the fragility of the line and shrinking the salient around Ypres to the very outskirts of the city.

Yet miraculously, Ypres did not fall. In a story that played itself out across the Western Front, the German offensives finally ran out of steam, not least because the French had largely recovered from the traumas of 1917, and were providing a coordinated counter-response to the German attacks, and also because the

Americans were adding their own weight to the Allied war effort by June of that year. The German offensives of March–May 1918 were actually last gasps. Soon it was the German turn to retreat, and this time the retreat did not stop until the war was finally brought to an end in November with an Armistice and an Allied victory.

For many post-war historians, the fact that the war ended with an Allied success in no way masks the grim realities of the Flanders campaign in 1917. As a final question on the merits or demerits of Third Ypres, we can ask: What would have happened had Britain not fought the battle?

German assault troops at Caporetto, on the Italian Front. Note the MG08/15 machine gun in the foreground, the German Army's poor attempt at creating a light machine gun.

A famous shot of stretcher bearers at Passchendaele; keeping wounds clean in such conditions was almost impossible, and blood poisoning and tetanus subsequently killed many casualties.

The central element of debate in this question is the state of the French Army in 1917. Following the Nivelle Offensive, the morale of the French forces was in a parlous state, and they were in no position to take any decisive offensive action at this stage of the war. It fell to the British and Commonwealth forces, and particularly those in Flanders, to keep the pressure on the Germans to prevent them taking advantage of the French situation. John Terraine, in his landmark book *The Road to Passchendaele* (required reading for anyone wanting detailed primary source documentation relating to Third Ypres), ends with a telling quotation from von Kuhl:

> Now that we know the circumstances of the situation in which the French Army found itself during the summer of 1917, there can be no doubt that in fact the stubbornness shown by the British bridged the crisis in France. The French Army gained time to restore itself and the German reserves were drawn to Flanders. The casualties which Britain sustained in defence of the Entente were not in vain.
>
> Von Kuhl, quoted in Terraine, *Road to Passchendaele*, p.342.

Coming from the mouth of an enemy commander, this statement is significant. As we noted at the beginning of this book, the battle for the Western Front was a unique conflict. With virtually no flank to turn, the Entente and German forces had to square off through bludgeoning frontal offensive and defensive strategies, all sung to the tune of rattling machine guns and endless artillery fire. The charge that Haig prosecuted the campaign of Third Ypres on days when progress was almost guaranteed to be negligible and bloody, probably sticks. The charge that Haig should have never launched the offensive in the first place requires more justification.

THE LEGACY

Having looked at some of the broader strategic issues relating to Third Ypres, we must bring matters back to the more personal level. In any war, the men who fight the battles might indeed have a grasp of the broader reasons behind why they fight, but in combat itself the focus is almost entirely on survival. The individual tragedies of the Battle of Passchendaele are legion, tens of thousands of men condemned to die in a pitiless landscape, a long way from the place that they call home.

Today, Passchendaele is a quiet and peaceful village in Flanders. Yet such is the violence of what occurred in the village and in Flanders a century ago, that the war has left an indelible mark. The most moving of these marks is almost certainly the Tyne Cot Cemetery, located near Zonnebeke. The name of the cemetery itself is taken from the title given to the German pillboxes; the name was applied by soldiers of the Northumberland Fusiliers, who felt the pillboxes looked like the 'Tyne Cots' (Tyneside cottages) in which many workers of that region lived. The main pillbox still stands in the cemetery, now adorned by the Cross of Sacrifice.

Tyne Cot is the largest Commonwealth cemetery in the world. Significantly enlarged following the Armistice, when remains were transferred from numerous other cemeteries in the region, today Tyne Cot features the graves of 11,956 Commonwealth servicemen, 8,369 of them unidentified.

Ranks of British graves at Tyne Cot, Britain's largest war cemetery. There are 11,956 Commonwealth servicemen buried in the graveyard.

The Cross of Sacrifice in Tyne Cot stands atop a German pillbox, one of many such features that proved stubborn against British assaults.

The elegant and moving Tyne Cot Memorial to the Missing then adds the names of a further 35,000 officers and men whose bodies were not recovered. Yet this overwhelming list is only actually a continuation. In Ypres stands the majestic Menin Gate Memorial to the Missing; designed by Sir Reginald Blomfield, it was unveiled on 24 July 1927. (The site was that of one of the city gates through which Allied troops passed to head up to the front line.) A cavernous Hall of Memory features dozens of stone panels, on which are carved the names of 54,896 Commonwealth soldiers who died at Ypres (although not those of New Zealanders or those from Newfoundland), but whose bodies remained undiscovered. In fact, the names at Menin Gate are actually those of men who

The Menin Gate at Ypres, and powerful act of remembrance to the tens of thousands of unidentified dead in Flanders.

died before 15 August 1917, and those of Tyne Cot are after this date. Although not all of the dead are from the Battle of Third Ypres, the scale of the memorials are an unsettling reminder of the human sacrifice poured into the Flanders soil between 1914 and 1918.

Other independent memorials are scattered around Flanders, creating a profound tapestry of loss across the Belgian landscape. Even today, so long after battles, haunting services are still held annually for the war dead, under the low clouds of a Flanders winter. No British veterans from the First World War era now survive, but the scale of what happened in Flanders all those years ago means that their experience will remain alive in peoples' minds for many generations to come.

ORDERS OF BATTLE

British Army Infantry Divisions and Brigades

Guards Division
1st Guards Brigade
2nd Guards Brigade
3rd Guards Brigade

1st Division
1st Brigade
2nd Brigade
3rd Brigade

3rd Division
8th Brigade
9th Brigade
76th Brigade

4th Division
10th Brigade
11th Brigade
12th Brigade

5th Division
13th Brigade
15th Brigade
95th Brigade

7th Division
20th Brigade
22nd Brigade
91st Brigade

8th Division
23rd Brigade
24th Brigade
25th Brigade

9th (Scottish) Division
26th Brigade
27th Brigade
S.A. Brigade

11th Division
32nd Brigade
33rd Brigade
34th Brigade

14th (Light) Division
41st Brigade
42nd Brigade
43rd Brigade

15th (Scottish) Division
44th Brigade
45th Brigade
46th Brigade

16th (Irish) Division
47th Brigade
48th Brigade
49th Brigade

17th (Northern) Division
50th Brigade
51st Brigade
52nd Brigade

18th (Eastern) Division
53rd Brigade
54th Brigade
55th Brigade

19th (Western) Division
56th Brigade
57th Brigade
58th Brigade

20th Division
59th Brigade
60th Brigade
61st Brigade

21st Division
62nd Brigade
64th Brigade
110th Brigade

23rd Division
68th Brigade
69th Brigade
70th Brigade

24th Division
17th Brigade
72nd Brigade
73rd Brigade

25th Division
4th Brigade
7th Brigade
75th Brigade

29th Division
86th Brigade
87th Brigade
88th Brigade

30th Division
21st Brigade
89th Brigade
90th Brigade

33rd Division
19th Brigade
98th Brigade
100th Brigade

34th Division
101st Brigade
102nd Brigade
103rd Brigade

35th Division
104th Brigade
105th Brigade
106th Brigade

36th (Ulster) Division
107th Brigade
108th Brigade
109th Brigade

37th Division
110th Brigade
111th Brigade
112th Brigade

38th (Welsh) Division
113th Brigade
114th Brigade
115th Brigade

39th Division
116th Brigade
117th Brigade
118th Brigade

41st Division
122nd Brigade
123rd Brigade
124th Brigade

42nd Division
125th Brigade
126th Brigade
127th Brigade

47th (1/2nd London) Division (TF)
140th Brigade
141th Brigade
142nd Brigade

48th (S. Midland) Division (TF)
143rd Brigade
144th Brigade
145th Brigade

49th (W. Riding) Division (TF)
146th Brigade
147th Brigade
148th Brigade

50th (Northumbrian) Division (TF)
149th Brigade
150th Brigade
151st Brigade

51st (Highland) Division
152nd Brigade
153rd Brigade
154th Brigade

55th (W. Lancs) Division (TF)
164th Brigade
165th Brigade
166th Brigade

56th (1/1st London) Division (TF)
167th Brigade
168th Brigade
169th Brigade

57th Division
170th Brigade
171st Brigade
172nd Brigade

58th Division
173rd Brigade
174th Brigade
175th Brigade

59th Division
176th Brigade
177th Brigade
178th Brigade

61st Division
182nd Brigade
183rd Brigade
184th Brigade

63rd (RN) Division
188th Brigade
189th Brigade
190th Brigade

66th Division
197th Brigade
198th Brigade
199th Brigade

1st Australian Division
1st (NSW) Brigade
2nd (Victoria) Brigade
9th (Queensland) Brigade

2nd Australian Division
5th (NSW) Brigade
6th (Victoria) Brigade
7th Brigade

3rd Australian Division
9th Brigade
10th Brigade
11th Brigade

4th Australian Division
4th Brigade
12th Brigade
13th Brigade

5th Australian Division
8th Brigade
14th (NSW) Brigade
15th (Victoria) Brigade

2nd Canadian Division
4th Brigade
5th Brigade
6th Brigade

4th Canadian Division
10th Brigade
11th Brigade
12th Brigade

1st Canadian Division
1st Brigade
2nd Brigade
3rd Brigade

3rd Canadian Division
7th Brigade
8th Brigade
9th Brigade

New Zealand Division
1st NZ Brigade
2nd NZ Brigade
3rd NZ Brigade

German Divisions and Regiments

Bavarian Ersatz Division
4th Bavarian Reserve
  Regiment
15th Bavarian Reserve
  Regiment
28th Ersatz Regiment

1st Bavarian Reserve Division
1st Bavarian Reserve
  Regiment
2nd Bavarian Reserve
  Regiment
3rd Bavarian Reserve
  Regiment

2nd Guard Division
71st Reserve Regiment
82nd Reserve
  Regiment
94th Reserve
  Regiment

3rd Reserve Division
2nd Reserve Regiment
34th Fusilier Regiment
49th Reserve
  Regiment

3rd Naval Division
1st Marine Regiment
2nd Marine Regiment
3rd Marine Regiment

4th Guard Division
5th Foot Regiment
5th Grenadier
  Regiment
93rd Reserve
  Regiment

4th Division
14th Regiment
49th Regiment
140th Regiment

4th Bavarian Division
5th Bavarian Regiment
5th Bavarian Reserve
  Regiment
9th Bavarian Regiment

5th Bavarian Division
1st Bavarian Regiment
19th Bavarian Regiment
21st Bavarian Regiment

5th Bavarian Reserve Division
7th Bavarian Reserve Regiment
10th Bavarian Reserve Regiment
12th Bavarian Reserve Regiment

6th Bavarian Division
6th Bavarian Regiment
10th Bavarian Regiment
13th Bavarian Regiment

6th Bavarian Reserve Division
16th Bavarian Reserve Regiment
17th Bavarian Reserve Regiment
20th Bavarian Reserve Regiment

7th Division
26th Regiment
163rd Regiment
393rd Regiment

8th Division
7th Regiment
93rd Regiment
153rd Regiment

8th Bavarian Reserve Division
18th Bavarian Reserve Regiment
19th Bavarian Reserve Regiment
22nd Bavarian Reserve Regiment
23rd Bavarian Reserve Regiment

9th Reserve Division
6th Reserve Regiment
19th Reserve Regiment
395th Regiment

9th Bavarian Reserve Division
3rd Ersatz Regiment
11th Bavarian Reserve Regiment
14th Bavarian Reserve Regiment

10th Ersatz Division
369th Regiment
370th Regiment
371st Regiment

10th Bavarian Division
6th Regiment
8th Bavarian Reserve Regiment
16th Bavarian Regiment

11th Reserve Division
10th Reserve Regiment
22nd Regiment
156th Regiment

11th Bavarian Division
13th Bavarian Reserve Regiment
3rd Regiment
22nd Regiment

12th Division
23rd Regiment
62nd Regiment
63rd Regiment

12th Reserve Division
22nd Reserve Regiment
38th Reserve Regiment
51st Reserve Regiment

15th Division
69th Regiment
160th Regiment
389th Regiment

15th Bavarian Division
30th Bavarian Regiment
31st Reserve Regiment
32nd Reserve Regiment

16th Division
28th Regiment
29th Regiment
68th Regiment

16th Bavarian Division
8th Bavarian Regiment
11th Bavarian Regiment
14th Bavarian Regiment

17th Division
75th Regiment
89th Grenadier Regiment
90th Fusilier Regiment

17th Reserve Division
16th Regiment
162nd Regiment
78th Reserve Regiment

18th Division
31st Regiment
85th Regiment
86th Fusilier Regiment

18th Reserve Division
31st Regiment
84th Regiment
86th Regiment

19th Reserve Division
73rd Reserve Regiment
78th Reserve Regiment
92nd Reserve Regiment

20th Division
77th Regiment
79th Regiment
92nd Regiment

22nd Division
82nd Regiment
83rd Regiment
167th Regiment

22nd Reserve Division
71st Reserve Regiment
82nd Reserve Regiment
167th Reserve Regiment

23rd Reserve Division
100th Reserve Grenadier Regiment
102nd Reserve Regiment
392nd Regiment

24th Division
133rd Regiment
139th Regiment
179th Regiment

25th Division
115th Guards Infantry
  Regiment
116th Infantry
  Regiment
117th Infantry
  Regiment

25th Reserve Division
83rd Reserve
  Regiment
118th Reserve
  Regiment
168th Regiment

26th Division
119th Grenadier
  Regiment
121st Regiment
125th Regiment

26th Reserve Division
119th Reserve
  Regiment
121st Reserve
Regiment
180th Regiment

27th Division
123rd Grenadier
  Regiment
120th Regiment
124th Regiment

32nd Division
102nd Regiment
103rd Regiment
177th Regiment

34th Division
67th Regiment
30th Regiment
145th Regiment

35th Division
61st Regiment
141st Regiment
176th Regiment

36th Division
5th Grenadier
  Regiment
128th Regiment
175th Regiment

38th Division
94th Regiment
95th Regiment
96th Regiment

39th Division
126th Regiment
132nd Regiment
172nd Regiment

40th Division
104th Regiment
134th Regiment
181st Regiment

41st Division
18th Regiment
148th Regiment
152nd Regiment

44th Reserve Division
205th Reserve
  Regiment
206th Reserve
  Regiment
208th Reserve
  Regiment

45th Reserve Division
210th Reserve
  Regiment
211th Reserve
  Regiment
212th Reserve
  Regiment

49th Reserve Division
225th Reserve
  Regiment
226th Reserve
  Regiment
228th Reserve
  Regiment

50th Reserve Division
229th Reserve Regiment
230th Reserve Regiment
231st Reserve Regiment

52nd Reserve Division
238th Reserve Regiment
239th Reserve Regiment
240th Reserve Regiment

54th Division
27th Reserve Regiment
84th Reserve Regiment
90th Reserve Regiment

54th Reserve Division
246th Reserve Regiment
248th Reserve Regiment

58th Division
106th Regiment
107th Regiment
103rd Reserve Regiment

79th Reserve Division
261st Reserve Regiment
262nd Reserve Regiment
263rd Reserve Regiment

111th Division
73rd Fusilier Regiment
76th Regiment
164th Regiment

119th Division
46th Regiment
58th Regiment
46th Reserve Regiment

121st Division
60th Regiment
7th Reserve Regiment
56th Reserve Regiment

183rd Division
184th Reserve Regiment
418th Reserve Regiment
440th Reserve Regiment

185th Division
28th Regiment
65th Regiment
161st Regiment

187th Division
187th Regiment
188th Regiment
189th Regiment

195th Division
6th Jäger Regiment
8th Jäger Regiment
233rd Reserve Regiment

199th Division
114th Regiment
357th Regiment
237th Reserve Regiment

204th Division
413th Regiment
414th Regiment
120th Reserve Regiment

207th Division
98th Reserve
  Regiment
209th Reserve
  Regiment
213th Reserve
  Regiment

208th Division
25th Regiment
185th Regiment
65th Reserve
  Regiment

214th Division
50th Regiment
358th Regiment
363rd Regiment

220th Division
190th Regiment
55th Reserve
  Regiment
999th Reserve
  Regiment

221st Division
41st Reserve Regiment
60th Reserve
  Regiment
1st Reserve Ersatz
  Regiment

227th Division
417th Regiment
441st Regiment
477th Regiment

231st Division
442nd Regiment
443rd Regiment
450th Regiment

233rd Division
448th Regiment
449th Regiment
450th Regiment

234th Division
451st Regiment
452nd Regiment
453rd Regiment

235th Division
454th Regiment
455th Regiment
456th Regiment

236th Division
457th Regiment
458th Regiment
459th Regiment

238th Division
463rd Regiment
464th Regiment
465th Regiment

239th Division
466th Regiment
467th Regiment
468th Regiment

240th Division
469th Regiment
470th Regiment
471st Regiment

FURTHER READING

Books

Birdwood, Field Marshal Lord, *Khaki and Gown: An Autobiography* (London: Ward Lock, 1942).

Cave, Nigel, *Passchendaele: The Fight for the Village* (Barnsley: Pen & Sword, 2007).

Charteris, Brigadier General John, *At G.H.Q.* (London: Cassell, 1931).

Doyle, Arthur Conan, *The British Campaign in France and Flanders 1915* (London: Hodder & Stoughton, 1919).

Edmonds James E., *Military Operations. France and Belgium, 1917* (Volume II) (London: HMSO, 1948).

Edmonds, James E. (ed.), *History of the Great War based on official documents by direction of the Historical Section of the Committee of Imperial Defence. Military Operations. France and Belgium, 1917:* [Vol. II] *Messines and Third Ypres (Passchendaele) 7 June–10 November* (London: HMSO, 1948).

Evans, Martin Marix, *Passchendaele: The Hollow Victory* (Barnsley, Pen & Sword, 2005).

Gibbs, Philip, *Adventures in Journalism* (London: Heinemann, 1923).

Gough, Hubert, *The Fifth Army* (London: Hodder & Stoughton, 1931).

Holt, Toni & Valmai, *Pocket Battlefield Guide to Ypres and Passchendaele* (Barnsley: Pen & Sword, 2011).

Horne, Charles F. (ed.), *Source Records of the Great War, Vol. II* (National Alumni, 1923).

McCarthy, Chris, *The Third Ypres: Passchendaele – The Day-by-Day Account* (London: Arms and Armour, 1995).

MacDonald, Lyn, *Passchendaele: The Story of the Third Battle of Ypres 1917* (London: Penguin, 2013).

Sheriff, Robert, *No Leading Lady* (London: Victor Gollancz Ltd, 1968).

Terraine, John, *The Road to Passchendaele* (London: Leo Cooper, 1971).

Useful Websites

www.firstworldwar.com – Excellent website featuring a large section on Third Ypres, including multiple primary sources.

www.cwgc.org/ypres/ – Commonwealth War Graves Commission site featuring histories of all the major battles at Ypres.

www.ww1battlefields.co.uk/flanders/passchendaele.html – Website explaining some of the key features to explore on a battlefield tour of Flanders.

Places to Visit

Flanders is replete with places of interest for the military historian; those given here are just a select few landmarks. Major & Mrs Holt's battlefield guide, given in the bibliography above, provides more in-depth guidance to the individual locations.

Gheluvelt village: on the N8, Menin Road. Numerous memorial plaques and monuments.

Langemarck: 4 miles (6km) north-east of Ypres. Includes a German cemetery and memorials to the 20th Light Division and 34th Division.

Passchendaele village: The heavily reconstructed village features a rebuilt church and numerous memorials and markers of battle sites, plus the Passchendaele New British Cemetery to the west. On the N303 south of the village, in Zonnebeke, is the Passchendaele Memorial 1917 Museum.

Sanctuary Wood: Features popular reconstructed trench systems (the Hill 62 Museum) and the Sanctuary Wood Cemetery.

Tyne Cot CWGC Cemetery and Memorial: Large CWGC war cemetery and memorial, located just south-west of Passchendaele.

Ypres: Numerous memorials, museums and cemeteries, including the majestic Menin Gate.

INDEX